IN THE LAND OF

SOLOMON

AND

SHEBA

Mimi LaFollette Summerskill

The Red Sea Press Inc.

Publishers & Distributors of Third World Books

P.O. Box 1982
Trenton, NJ 08607

P.O. Box 48
Asmara, ERITREA

The Red Sea Press, Inc.

Publishers & Distributors of Third World Books

11-D Princess Road   P. O. Box 48
Lawrenceville, NJ 08648   Asmara, ERITREA

Copyright © 2002 Mimi LaFollette Summerskill

Library of Congress Catalog-in-Publication Data

Summerskill, Mimi LaFollette.
    In the Land of Solomon and Sheba / Mimi LaFollette Summerskill.
      p. cm.
    ISBN 1-56902-092-2 -- ISBN 1-56902-093-0 (pbk.)
    1. Ethiopia--Description and travel. 2. Summerskill, Mimi LaFollette--Homes and haunts--Ethiopia. I. Title.

    DT378.3 .S86 2001
    963.07--dc21   2001031742

Dedication

This book is dedicated to Haile Seilasse's children and grandchildren

Table of Contents

1   ፩

Moving To Ethiopia

"Mrs. Summerskill? This is Seble Desta calling."

"Yes, Mrs. Desta. How can I help you? "

"Mrs. Summerskill, Mimi, it is Princess Seble--from Ethiopia."

It was February of 1992, and I had not seen Seble and her sisters for twenty-one years. They had been imprisoned for fourteen of those years and only recently released. That I had read, but we had no idea where they were living.

"My mother, Princess Ruth, and I are in Washington D.C. We would love to see you. Ruth is going to live in London, but is here for a month. Yes, I have seen all six of my children. Some live in New York, and the youngest boy is at Brown University."

"How did you ever find me?"

"An Ethiopian friend in Washington D. C. said that Dr. Summerskill lived near Princeton. I called information."

Long after Princess Seble hung up I sat, holding the phone in my hand, I sat in the winter sun at the kitchen breakfast table of our log house, awash with memories of those beautiful grandaughters of Emperor Haile Selassie I and the wonder of our brief years living on the high plateau of Ethiopia, a country known in the ancient world as Abyssinia.

John Summerskill and I were married just a few days when we boarded the great ocean liner Leonardo da Vinci in New York harbor. We were headed for John's new job in East Africa's mysterious kingdom Ethiopia. The land of the Queen of Sheba. John was my Solomon, and I, his Sheba. We were deeply in love and old enough to know how precious that was! John had resigned as president of San Francisco State University a few months before, leaving the turmoil of the sixties and his enemy, Governor Reagan, to fend for themselves. The year was 1968.

Three months earlier we had paid a brief visit to Ethiopia. Not yet married (John's divorce not yet final), we pretended that we were, and it was many months before the Ford Foundation people confessed they had known all along of our subterfuge. "The president of Haile Selassie University would like to meet with you before we confirm your appointment as his advisor." So spoke a Ford Foundation official who had approached John with that exotic job offer. "Could you take a week before graduation and fly over to Addis Ababa?"

John had been a professor and later vice-president of Cornell before going out to become president of San Francisco State University. The Ford Foundation was looking for someone who had been both a professor and an administrator, someone crazy enough to think living in Ethiopia for two or three years would be a rewarding adventure. John's problems at San Francisco State had been so publicized, notably from a story in Life magazine, that a number of unusual job offers came his way and two of them were with the Ford Foundation. One job was in Ethiopia; the other opportunity was in Nigeria. It was almost like running away, leaving the student problems in San Francisco, the radical Students for a Democratic Society (SDS), the Black Nationalist movement, and the pressures on universities sparked by the Vietnam war. John had marched in a peace parade against the Vietnam War, marched up Market Street in San Francisco with his young son John Paul on his shoulders. That march was much publicized, and Governor Reagan was furious. It had become a big bore for us to see John's picture every single day on the front page of both the Chronicle (the morning paper that supported John's actions) and the Examiner (the very conservative paper that didn't).

On our big scouting trip we flew to Athens, Greece, where we boarded Ethiopian Airlines for the six-hour trip south to Addis Ababa. John went to meet Emperor Haile Selassie and President Kassa (Seble's husband and the university's president.) I looked for houses we might live in--if John were asked and chose to go. We flew back to New York so that John could give a commencement address, unaware of the consternation our departure for Ethiopia had caused in some quarters.

"What do you mean, John Summerskill has gone to Ethiopia? He can't. He's our graduation speaker!"

Esther Rausenbusch, president of Sarah Lawerence College looked at her secretary in amazement. The secretary held up a paper.

"It's here--in the New York Times this morning. He left yesterday. And graduation is just a week away."

Somehow it never occurred to John that Mrs. Rausenbush should be notified of his academic

3

interview halfway round the world. We knew we'd be back on time and with a few hours to spare. The speech was duly delivered. We flew back to San Francisco, where we faced the anguish of our about-to-be-moved-to-Africa children.

It was in late summer of 1968 that we finally set sail for Ethiopia, via New York and Genoa, on the Leonardo da Vinci. From Rome we picked up Ethiopian Airlines and flew south. We took with us eight flokati rugs from Greece, a barrel of china from Portugal, and a hundred or more books, clothes and my two youngest children: Wendy 15 and Robert 13, who went kicking and screaming. Robert plotted for weeks, seeking to delay the inevitable. A group of Wendy's friends in Menlo Park, California (where I had lived for twenty four years with my five offspring) presented us with a petition, amid floods of tears. "You can't take her away and expose her to lions and snakes and other tropical horrors."

The Leonardo was one of the old-fashioned luxury liners that plied the Atlantic in those days. Because of my previous occupation, operating a travel agency for a number of years on the Stanford University campus and making travel arrangements for some major corporations, we were given one of the ship's two elegant suites. We had our own salon and two staterooms--each with bath. We were astounded as the steward opened our stateroom door with a flourish, "John, look at the flowers!" There were enormous bouquets everywhere, flowers from deck to deck--all for Mrs. Wright (my married name until the marriage to John two days earlier). We lost most of the flowers, however, when the chief steward discovered our suite was occupied by Miriam LaFollette Wright and the other luxury suite by Mrs. Frank Lloyd Wright.

Being aboard the Leonardo da Vinci it felt like I had died and gone to heaven. For John it meant no more hassles with politicians, no more late night meetings with student groups. For me, no more household decisions and no more good-bye parties. Even Robert and Wendy, who did not leave their stateroom for the first three days of the ten-day voyage, ended up having a great adventure aboard that handsome ship. At dinner on our first night, an attractive man walked over to our table.

"Hello, I'm Richard Widmark. You're the Summerskills, aren't you? I just stopped by to tell you how much I admired you, Dr. Summerskill, when you were up against Ronald Reagan."

Mr. Widmark told us he had known "Ronnie" in Hollywood for some twenty years and was not an admirer of the actor turned governor. The trustees of the California Colleges and Universities had had a "hearing" about John. It was close to an inquisition, challenging his handling of the student unrest on the campus. Although John had not called the police to the campus, he and the police shared a "hot line" during that period. "If police show up, John, it will escalate the whole thing. You be the judge. We'll stand by, and if you need us we can be there in five minutes." So spoke San Francisco's police chief.

One enormous "plus" for John and me was that we had a month before he had to report for duty in Addis Ababa, "We can have four weeks on Ios," John announced. "That should soften the horror of our move for Wendy and Robert." So off we flew to Athens, where we took the all-day ferry to Ios island, just a few miles north of the famous volcanic island of Santorini (Thera).

In the summer of 1965, I had chartered a handsome racing schooner for three months and sailed with my children in Greek waters. Three weeks into the sail, I fell in love with Ios, purchased some land and my farm neighbors built us a sprawling stone house. Our whole family had gone to Ios the summer of '67, and so in '68, as we sailed into the deep harbor of Ios, it felt like "going home." The whitewashed houses of the village wrapped the conical-shaped hill behind the harbor. We took donkeys up to the village, passing by thirteen Dutch-style windmills that stood along the high ridge of Ios. And so on down the rough path to the long, curved beach of Milopotas--and our house. What wondrous days of peace, with no phone, no electricity! Just lazy days, nights spent under our great cones of mosquito netting and endless hours floating in the Aegean day-dreaming about our new life in Ethiopia.

All too soon it was September, and we boarded the old island ferry for the long ride back to Athens, stopping on the islands of Naxos (famous from Venetian days) and Paros. The first part of our plane trip south from Athens was over the Mediterranean and the large island of Crete, then up the Nile River, which is flanked by green. "One can only imagine when the whole of Egypt was wooded land instead of desert, back in the days when it was a Coptic Christian country, with great influence on Ethiopia."

"The river is still the life-line of Egypt," my spouse answered, as he leaned across me to peer out the small oval of the airline window. "Look below, there are the peaks of the Semien mountains. We must be over Ethiopia."

On Ethiopian Airlines the lovely, slender flight attendants who served us looked like the relief drawings of Nefertiti in the temple at Abu Simbal in Egypt. They were dressed in sheer white cotton with a colored border around the bottom of the skirt. "I wish you could have been with me, John, when I spent those three days on the Nile and at Abu Simbal before it was moved for the dams." At the airport, before departure, John and I had been introduced to our co-pilot, who was Ethiopian. In those days the TWA pilots were Americans, part of the staff who were training Ethiopians how to run an airline--from soup to nuts. The young co-pilot bowed slightly to us as he shook hands. This gracious custom of bowing we came to admire and emulate. When greeting a friend, one first bows slightly and then begins an extended ritual of kissing cheeks, alternating sides.

It was dawn when we landed on the 5,000 foot plateau above the Red Sea, where Ethiopia's second largest city, Asmara, is located. Disembarking in the warm, clear air of early morning we noticed a field of grain being harvested at one side of the runway. There must have been a hundred men and women in a long line, each with a simple short scythe in hand. This human harvest machine moved slowly and rhythmically through the golden grain. In the airport we each had a cup of espresso, our first coffee in coffee country. We soon learned that coffee was first grown in Ethiopia, in the province of Kaffa--hence called "coffee" as it became a popular drink all over the world.

"This is your captain speaking," the soft Texas drawl reassured. "We are about to leave the mountainous region of northern Ethiopia and will soon be flying over the great Shoan plateau in the center of the country. Off the right wing you will see the gorge of the Blue Nile." It was magnificent. The "little rains" of spring had turned the fields green, and the plateau was dotted with gray-green groves of eucalyptus. We could see two of the lakes beyond the Rift Valley and wondered at the earth's massive upheavals that form the dramatic cut of "the Rift." Beginning in Saudi Arabia, the Rift Valley

7

runs under the Red Sea, sinks below sea level in eastern Ethiopia, rises to 5,000 feet and then, as it continues on down into Kenya and Uganda, fills with volcanic lakes and hills of exotic shapes.

"Look at the fields below, Mimi. They are solid yellow like the rape fields in Scotland." Our plane was circling to the south of the capital, Addis Ababa, and above fields of yellow mescal daisies that cover the countryside in September. All four of us peered down on the exotic landscape that was to be our new home.

We could not move in to our Ambo Road house in the Gulele district of Addis without furniture, so we took up residence at the old Ghion Hotel across from the emperor's stables and not too far from the Addis Ababa airport. The hotel looks down a slope to the streets of Addis and across to the tree-covered hills that ring the city.

Driving up the curving road to the hotel, amid lawns and trees, our driver told us that the old part of the Ghion Hotel was built by the emperor as his guest house. "And there," he gestured toward a low building on the hotel grounds, "are the emperor's stables." Slender grooms dressed in white Jodhpur pants were walking several magnificent horses around the paddock.

"What is that handsome building across the street?" John pointed.

"Ah, sir, that is the Jubilee Palace, where our emperor lives."

On our first day in Ethiopia, we watched an enormous surging crowd from our hotel room. It was the jubilant feast of Maskal in early September. The emperor's guards lined the road stretching from the airport (they did this, we discovered, for all "important visitors," and several had arrived for the Maskal celebration.) Each soldier-guard wore a lion's mane.

8

Yes, a real lion's mane, a sort of skin cap was underneath with the mane standing out in every direction (son Robert soon acquired one), and each soldier held a long wooden spear tipped with a metal spearhead. The soldiers were dressed in white, again with jodhpur-like trousers. With a backdrop of green lawns and blooming jacaranda trees, the whole scene a setting for an opera, and I was the heroine.

Men, women, and children, all dressed in white with shamas (a long loosely woven scarf of white cotton which is worn wrapped around the head and shoulders), pushed toward Maskal Square, where the religious ceremony took place. The men hurled their flaming chibos, or torches, into a great blazing bonfire. With the women trilling and singing it was an exuberant crowd, and the Addis Ababa fire department had their hands full extinguishing fires all over the place, fires accidentally started by passing torches.

John and I decided to join the celebration, and we were soon engulfed by happy, chanting Ethiopians who paid no attention to us whatsoever. Suddenly horror swept over me. The man pressing past John was a leper, and his decaying arm was against John's. We had not seen leprosy before--but would do so many times before leaving Ethiopia.

The following morning a car from the university picked us up, and we drove up the gentle slope of Entoto Mountain on a broad, tree-lined avenue. "The Emperor's palace is on your left," the driver said. "He is in residence since the flag is flying." Green, red and yellow strips fluttered brightly in the clear, African air. "And on the right is the OAU. We call it African Hall, and I suppose you know it is the headquarters for the countries of Africa. It is our United Nations, Organization of African Unity." We had not known. So up and up we drove, curving around the huge grounds of Menelek's palace surrounded with an elegant wrought iron fence, past the parliament building, around several kilos (roundabouts), and on to the Haile Selassie I University. The entrance gates were imposing, and only then did we learn that the main building of Ethiopia's national university had been the palace of Ras (Lord) Makonnen, the emperor's father, and that Haile Selassie had given it to the country in 1961 when the university was established. Across the avenue stood another imposing set of gates that led in to the compound of the Embassy of the United States of America. Good neighbors.

While John interviewed I went to the top floor of the old palace to visit the Museum of the Institute of Ethiopian Studies, wandering among the well-displayed artifacts. I was soon to learn that nearly everything in the museum is still in use in the country today, and that fact alone makes it unique in the museum world. I was fascinated by the furniture, having no idea that most of the pieces I admired, like Jima chairs and basket tables, would soon be part of my own household in Addis. But it was the cases of icons and crosses that held me spellbound.

The crosses in the university museum vary, from tiny ones that were, and are still worn around the neck, to large processional crosses. These are intricately cut from iron or brass and sometimes etched. Others are carved from wood. Some of the crosses were beautifully wrought, while others were fairly crude. That afternoon the larger crosses were much in evidence as we watched a funeral procession. Each of the white-robed priests, slender and handsome in their turbans, had an assistant who held an ornate velvet umbrella over the priest's head.

At the museum I had been lucky enough to talk with Richard Pankhurst (son of the famous suffragette, Sylvia Pankhurst) and one of the two curators who had collected the contents of the museum on countless trips through the countryside of his adopted country.

John toured his small office in the old palace building, and we returned to the hotel. During the next weeks John began to know the various professors (from nineteen different nations) at the university, and I launched myself to furnishing our barren but handsome new home on the Ambo Road. Our adventure in Ethiopia had begun.

2   ę̄

A House Is Not A Home— Even With Lion Cages

The lion cages had no lions, the aviary had no birds, and the house had no furniture, but what a house! Sitting on an embankment and surrounded by English lawns bordered with hollyhocks and roses, the house was dramatic and proud as it sat against a gentle hill, well above the surrounding neighborhood. To the left of the house was a large lawn that became our croquet court. When Wendy and Robert came home from school on their two-hour lunch break, we often had a rousing croquet match.

After visitors had been bowed through our iron gates by Asafa and his cutlass (another Asafa guarded at night, hunkering in the tiny round guard house next to the gates), they passed through the grove of eucalyptus trees just inside the iron gate of our compound. Eucalyptus had become one of the most important crops of Ethiopia. The leaves of that lovely, fragrant tree are fuel for the tiny cook stoves that most people use. The straight, slender trunks of the eucalyptus seem to have many uses in framing a turkel (thatched hat) home, constructing fences or ladders and even beds, and fuelling fires for heating and cooking. Our eucalyptus grove was invaded every day as neighborhood people came to gather leaves for cooking.

Our new home was built on the outskirts of Addis Ababa before World War II. It was built in the mid-1930s in the Gulele district of Addis on the Ambo Road. Its former owner was Blatengeta (Lord) Hirui, who had been the foreign minister to Haile Selassie in the early days of the emperor's reign. That elegant looking small man was always dressed to perfection and with a newly cut rose in his lapel. He and his rotund wife lived next door. There is a famous story about Blatengeta Hirui. One day he was seen herding twelve donkeys up the main street of Addis. Quickly surrounded by a curious crowd, he told them, "These donkeys represent the emperor's ministers." This was during the period when Haile Selassie was shifting ministers practically on a weekly basis. The old man could get away with such impudence as he had been in exile, in Bath, England, with the emperor in the mid-30's.

Addis Ababa was growing rapidly by the time we arrived, and the city already had grown to surround our walled compound of three acres. Many of these families in our neighborhood, thousands of them, lived in mud and dung chica houses with tin roofs, while some lived in village-like turkels that were round and usually had only one room. There was constant pedestrian traffic past our compound, Ethiopian men, women, and children walking the muddy road to market or to school or to the nearest tej (liquor) house. They were proud, handsome people, always courteously correct with us, the only foreigners in their midst.

Our house was a landmark in the Gulele district, as for many years it was the embassy for a number of governments until abandoned to itinerant foreigners.

Visitors to our home parked below the house, next to the lion cages and in front of the twenty or so brick steps that led up to the front porch. Two stone towers connected the porch with the large square house behind. The spacious rooms, with their high ceilings, had long windows, handsome hard wood floors and four fireplaces. Although close to the equator, Addis is located in the Semien Mountains at an altitude of 8,000 feet. We soon found that we had leaks in our tin roof and often had to run for a pot when either the "little rains" or the torrential "big rains" hit every year.

Besides having no furniture, our wondrous new home was without storage. Spacious rooms, yes, but no cupboards, no closets, no shelves. One could identify the kitchen, as it had a dinky metal sink attached to a wall. Yet that handsome house had two enormous bathrooms, fortunately complete with fixtures. A huge white bathtub dominated the expanse of white tile. We added two potted banana trees, one in each corner for color and amusement. With a limited supply of hot water we would fill the large tub. John would pour us each a scotch, and we'd climb in, gentleman John taking the faucet end. "Do either of you children want to use our bath?" Often they did.

Our monthly water bill soon informed us that we owed over $1100 dollars for water. Blata Hirui's wife came over, "I have checked all your faucets for leaking." John was quietly amused that a few drips could be hundreds of dollars. It was all solved when the meter reader confessed that he had simply written down numbers at home, instead of actually reading the meters in his district. All of our neighbors had equally interesting bills.

We had found our house through Charles Leithead, a doctor from Scotland who had headed the general hospital in Addis for twenty years. After living many years in the Gulele district, the Leitheads decided to rent a farm outside of the city. We were very lucky in our timing, for spacious houses, unless in the foreign compounds, were hard to come by, and we were eager to live in an Ethiopian neighborhood.

"Where to start, John? I guess with beds and maybe a servant or two." We sat, my love and I, in the gardens of the Ghion Hotel, watching our children cavort in the pool.

"Someone is going to have to drive Wendy and Robert to the British school, so I guess we better interview drivers first. The Leitheads say there is very little furniture to be had in Addis, so I guess almost everything will have to be made."

It is a challenge to furnish a house in a city where there is no furniture for sale. The exception was for Mosvolds--a small, Swedish store selling low couches, chairs and beds, all made of a light colored wood. I felt like a pioneer as I set out to make our great mansion with its high-ceilinged rooms livable. I was happy. Though, as formerly stated, John and I were just married (in our forties with eight children between us), everyone at the university took it for granted that it had always been "John and Mimi." As far as we were concerned it always had been. We were very much in love and knew we were blessed.

After purchasing beds for the family, I visited an Indian man who made furniture. He made us three oblong tables, a square leg in each corner, and he stained the wood a rich dark brown. I put one of the tables in the middle of our vast dining room and one against each end wall, where they could collect junk yet be moved to make a very long table when needed. The Gulele house dining room was larger than the living room and, with its twelve feet high ceilings and large fireplace, an especially neat room--if it could be furnished with any originality. What were we to do for chairs? "John, do you remember that unusual black chair we saw at the British Embassy? I think it comes from Ethiopia." The British ambassador's wife told me she had gotten the chair at the market place. It's called a Jima chair."

Jima is a town about 200 miles southwest of Addis Ababa in Kaffa province. An important village man in that part of Ethiopia would own a Jima chair. It takes a huge log to produce the Jima chair, as it is carved all in one piece. Three cleverly carved legs come off the concave bottom, which is shaped to accommodate the human bottom. The chair back is straight, carved in a geometric pattern and the back is about the height of the occupants head. Lesser mortals in a Kaffa village sit on Jima stools, which again have three legs and a concave seat. The stools, of course, are much lower in height than the chairs, and have no backs. The problem is the position of the three legs on both the chairs and stools. One chair leg is directly under the spine, with the second leg out to the left, the third to the right. One night a heavy-set guest at our dinner table sat down too far forward and the chair tipped her off and under the table. A true drama ensued as the lady was retrieved and placed on the center of her chair. From that night on John announced to all dinner guests, "When you sit down put your bottom well back!"

For the next three months our driver, Yeardow, and I took many trips to the vast market fields in Addis. It soon got became known that I wanted to buy Jima chairs. Acquiring twelve Jima chairs turned out to be a complicated matter. Every time Yeardow and I visited the market "chair shopping," a large crowd gathered round to help and advise as I tried out the chairs. It seemed important to find chairs of vaguely the same height. After all, one couldn't have one guest sitting a foot below his other partner to the left or right. Some of the chairs forced the sitter to lean slightly forward, as if in an inquiring position. The backs of other chairs tended to lull one into slumber land. The chairs are made of some exotic hardwood and, with years of rancid butter rubbed into them, are nearly black in color. Jima chairs are now considered objects of art, and when visiting the Smithsonian National Museum of African Art in Washington D. C. and seeing those handsome chairs, I can now say, knowledgeably, "Oh, yes, a Jima chair." Our chairs, John's and mine, have been distributed, all except four, among our many offspring. A handsome memory of life on the high plateau of ancient Abyssinia.

"End tables? We have to have some place to put a drink, a book, or some flowers. What about end tables, Mimi?" John asked. Near Addis was a marble works of sorts, carrying what one might call "designer marble." There they made things for the noble families. As in any marble yard, rough-hewn pieces stood on end, flat soldiers tilted toward one another for support. We chose five pieces, two quite small; the largest was coffee table size. One side had been finished, not shiny finished, but at least sufficiently polished so the buyer could see the colors. Bases? Ah, yes, on Churchill Street was the ironmonger, an Armenian whose artifacts we had noticed in front of his shop. That clever soul made us five bases with twisted wrought-iron legs and a triangular frame top to support our marble pieces.

Thirteen-year-old Robert took on the job of making lamps. John and Robert had rewired our house during our first month in Addis, so Robert was already knowledgeable about the electrics. We bought a number of wooden head rests that are about ten inches in height, the tops shaped to hold one's neck. (It's hard to believe a human can sleep on one.) Some are of solid wood, with a fine patina from use over the decades, others have a base and a slender necklike piece that supports the headrest. Robert drilled holes up from the bottom in each of the headrests. The holes were the size of copper piping Yeardow had located. A local garage threaded the protruding ends of pipe, and we fitted light fixtures on the top, Woolworth fixtures purchased on a trip back to America. Shaping heavy wire for shades, I wound yarn around and around and around the frames, a different color for each room. Handsome, homemade lamps.

We had barely furnished our dwelling, that fall of 1968, when we were informed that Secretary of State Bill Rogers would be visiting Addis, and "we hope you will entertain the secretary and his wife for breakfast." The protocol officer at the American Embassy suggested that we invite a number of Ethiopian professors to attend, and that breakfast be served at 8:10. So, we were launched socially!

3

Friends, Servants and Baboons in the Aviary

The iron doors to our lion cages were always open. Built of brick by an Italian general during the occupation of Ethiopia before World War II, with steel-barred roofs and sides, the cages held lions until the British soldiers rode victoriously into Addis Ababa in 1940. So the Brits liberated the country from Mussolini and the lions from their cages. These were impressive cages, just like in a zoo. They stood to one side of the large parking area in front of our house. It made me sad to have those empty lion cages as well as an empty aviary. The aviary, covering an enormous area of our lawn had a wire mesh dome. Then one day the aviary acquired a tenant. He was a Semien Mountain baboon.

John brought him home one noon, having paid a young street boy a small amount of money. "The boy was abusing the poor baboon. Couldn't we keep him in the aviary?" Mr. Semien became John's devoted friend.

Often, as we sat between the stone towers on our porch having a drink, the baboon would sit close to John and carefully inspect his arms for insects, looking up at the master, chatting all the while. John, being quite fair, had relatively hairless arms, but that did not deter Mr. Semien. Our new pet was from the mountains and was long, lean and dark brown, with an almost human leer. Because we did not want him to wander, we attached a long rope onto a chain and anchored the whole to a tree near the house. At night he lived in the aviary. Mr. Semien, who would sometimes get loose during the day, seemed to delight in the horrible noise his chain made as he raced across our corrugated metal roof. We usually had a stalk of bananas leaning against one wall of our vast kitchen. He would pull one off and, in a series of grunts and squeaks, plead with someone to peel the fruit. Racing to the deep casement windows in the dining room, which were usually open, Mr. Semien would lean against the casing and slowly eat his delicacy. John and I took care of the Leithead's baby girl when Mama Leithead went into the hospital to deliver baby number two. Blond Alison was a year-and-a-half old and would sit on the throw rug in front of our dining room fireplace, her back rim rod straight, feet out in front as she too ate a banana. The baboon and the baby would glower at each other the while. During Wendy and Robert's long school lunch hour, our family often had a croquet game on our cropped lawn. Mr. Semien loved to hunker under a Norfolk pine and watch. Sometimes he would stretch out on the grass, hoping Wendy would tickle his tummy.

One day tragedy struck. During the night Mr. Semien got his chain wrapped around his neck, and in the morning we found him hanged in his aviary. All the servants joined us in an emotional funeral service.

Servants. A whole way of life I was to discover. We were the servants of the staff just as much as they were of us. Interdependent, shoulder-to-shoulder we worked. Each of us had responsibilities and little powers. It started with John -- Gitoch (Amharic for the "master of a house") was, in the end responsible for us all. His duties varied from being the final authority in disputes (always following the senior servants recommendations) to signing on as father for Edjigia's brother and for a neighborhood blind boy. Oh, I loved it! Having been a single parent for nearly nine years, I could now say, "Gitoch will decide." Of course, John took a lot of teasing from Wendy and Robert, but nevertheless it was a serious part of our lives, John being master.

The home guard, Asafa

In Ethiopia poor people might beg you for food, for a place to stay, and especially for a job. So we had a cook and a maid and a driver and a gardener and a groom for

23

the horses and a day guard and a night guard. John did not allow anyone to come on Sundays--even the guards-- so we had one day of quiet.

"Mama, Mama, come quick. Asafa's wife, she have baby," Edjigia kept calling at our bedroom door. It was four in the morning. "She no want Gitoch---she want you." Asafa and his fourteen-year-old wife lived in our servants cottages, which accommodated four families. Asafa harassed John constantly: "If you buy me a rifle I can guard you better." John bought him a whistle instead. "Blow the whistle Asafa, and I will come help you immediately." Asafa, chagrined, bought himself a curved sword, though he did keep the whistle.

The nanny, Edjigia

Asafa was not on hand, as moments after Edjigia's call we were in the car--Edjigia, the child-wife and I, racing for the hospital. I had stopped only long enough to call Dr. Leithead. "Go! I will meet you there," he ordered.

24

Haile Selassie Hospital had an excellent reputation. One of Haile Selassie's daughters had been a nurse there until her premature death. Our little group was ushered into the dressing room, and the nurse had the young girl lie down and lifted her dress to expose a very large and round belly. "There is no sign of labor," the nurse said, although the young woman was obviously in pain. The diagnosis was acute gastroenteritis. Armed with medication we dragged ourselves home, only to repeat the whole procedure a few weeks later when real labor began.

Edjigia was our exquisitely beautiful mamita (nanny). Even though we had no little children, she was mamita to Robert and Wendy. There was a day when we almost lost her, as she nearly died from ignorance. We raced her to the hospital, where they pumped her stomach, and Edjigia confessed to Doctor Leithead that she had drunk turpentine to get rid of an unwanted fetus. Charles Leithead gave Edjigia a short course in anatomy, explaining that the fetus was not in her stomach. "You must learn to trust the doctors and not listen to old wives tales." Edjigia already had a son. He lived with her mother in a village some fifty miles from Addis. The problem was that Edjigia had no husband. She spoke of the young soldier who had fathered the baby as "my husband" but many times told Wendy "we not have real wedding." Edgie's parents were from different tribes, and that created marriage problems.

Wendy and Edjigia talked endlessly. Two flawlessly beautiful females who were deeply bonded. Edjigia was half Galla and half Amharic, and that in itself made some confusion in the mores she lived by. In her village marriages were arranged between the families after the two young people made known their intent. The perspective groom would then make presents of animals to the father of the girl and brought specified gifts to the perspective bride--a dress, jewelry. Village elders presided at marriages, drew up the contract, and watched to see the marriage properly consummated. The girl, however, is supposedly a virgin. We were told many horror stories of girls, not only having their clitoris removed (it was an old custom in the country), but of girls who had their hymen restored. A girl does not give up her maiden name in Ethiopia, and the marriage can be dissolved with complaints from either partner. The village chimagli (elders) who presided over the wedding then also preside over the divorce. Property is returned, and the two parties can make a fresh start. John and I attended a few weddings, and the most fascinating part to me was the celebration afterwards when all elders sat in a row, and the bride and groom passed in front, kissing the knees of each elder.

Robert had his own special relationship with Edjigia, always making her laugh. When my youngest son was tiny, I had tickled his arm briefly when I tucked him bed at night. Robert persuaded Edjigia to continue the practice, so every night Edjigia tickled Robert's arm until he dozed off. Our first summer in Addis Ababa saw my oldest son Richard arrive to stay with us, desperately ill with infectious hepatitis, contracted when he visited his brother Bill, who was serving in the Peace Corps in Upper Volta, later Bokino Fasso. Edjigia slept on the floor at the foot of Richard's bed, unwilling to leave him unattended. Richard was indeed desperately ill, with the highest bilirubin count Dr. Leithead had ever seen in anyone who survived in East Africa, and Edjigia was his nurse, day and night.

The first servant we employed was Ato Walkie, our cook. A dignified older man, Ato Walkie lived with wife and seven offspring, in his own home near our compound. He was the arbitrator of servant disputes and definitely a leader. Ato Walkie had a greying pompadour, the features of a Roman Senator, and his back was as straight as a chair. He was a splendid cook, the only problem being that he wanted to cook more than we wanted to eat. Sometimes the servants would group on the front lawn in front of the porch and perform tribal dances, chanting and singing along. On these days Ato Walkie would sit on the steps as an observer.

Yeardow, our driver, looked like the captain of the *H.M.S Queen Elizabeth* in his royal blue uniform. He hated our two-door Volkswagen station wagon, especially when he was surrounded by big sedans at embassy functions. Nevertheless, he was a boon to my shopping life, as he advised and carried. I loved learning small bits of gossip from him. One day he informed me, "Madam, you know they say there is a man on the moon now. It is not true. There is no way to get to the moon."

There was the day that all of Robert's clothes disappeared. Ato Walkie was sure it was an inside job. The whole neighborhood was concerned. A delegation came to our gate, and they were adamant: No one in the neighborhood would steal from our house. Our cook offered to help. He asked John to go with him across town to the house where our driver lived (the driver before Yeardow). The cook went in for a minute or two and came out with Robert's clothes. "I told his wife her husband would go to jail, and she gave me the clothes."

My favorite servant friend, next to Edjigia, was Daba, but his hiring was fraught with problems. Since we had a horse barn, complete with showers for the horses, Robert and I decided we wanted to have horses as we both loved riding and knew we could buy two western saddles from a departing American army officer. "After all, I was queen of a western rodeo when I was young--and now I have a chance to ride again--in style." An English family, the Sanfords, had long been in Ethiopia, living on a ranch outside of Addis. When Daba applied for the job as groom for our newly purchased horses, he presented a reference from Mrs. Sanford extolling his virutes and talent with horses. I called Mrs. Sanford. She was incredulous and immediately drove over to our house. "Daba, how could you show these people a reference I wrote for another man?!"

Daba was ready: "It's much too good a letter to be used by only one man, Madam."

Mrs. Sanford told us that Daba was a good worker and honest but had little experience with horses. On instinct I said, "John, let's hire him. Look at his face." Mrs. Sanford relayed the news in the Galla dialect. Daba advanced toward me. "Don't move, don't look down...," Mrs Sanford advised. Daba bent and kissed my feet as I stared at the African sky in embarrassment. Later, when we learnt a bit more about customs, I would not have been so nonplussed. Often at weddings and other social functions, Ethiopians would kiss the knees of their elders as they sat in a line at a social event.

It wasn't just the servants who took care of us; the whole neighborhood did. Late one afternoon a cry went up, "Fire!" Ethiopians converged on our house from all directions. It was the living room ceiling. Although Addis Ababa is only 8 degrees north of the equator, the altitude is 8,000 feet, so we used our fireplaces many winter evenings. Somehow, one night, the heat seeped from the chimney into the ceiling, and there was lots of smoke and some flames. Our neighbors put out the fire with brooms and water and disappeared as quickly as they came. John and I felt deeply grateful for living in a community where we all took care of one another.

We soon became aware that most of our educated Ethiopian friends had servants who, as far as we could see, lived in virtual slavery. Slavery officially ended in Ethiopia in 1927, by decree from the emperor. It had existed in many forms for centuries in Ethiopia, the slaves coming from conquered tribes. In more recent years, the Christian Amhars in northern and central Ethiopia would raid the tribes to the south--often the Galla--for their slaves. One day Wendy, coming home particularly distressed, complained: "When I visit Marie, her servant is dressed in rags, sort of grey and dirty. It seems so strange. She puts starchy white clothes on Marie." One day while I was waiting for my tennis lesson, I asked a young Ethiopian matron why she did not buy a new uniform for her mamita. "If I do she might not know her place."

Sometimes one saw the other side of the coin. My friend Salamaweit (wife of Aklilu--the president of the university) took me to a pleasant, airy room in her home. "I want you to meet our oldest servant." There sat an ancient, miniature lady of 108 years! "She raised all of our children, and when she turned 80 she became a nun." And from that day on the old servant had lived with Salamaweit. "Each day she washes and irons her white dress," Salamaweit told me as the tiny lady got up from her bed, kissed my hand and smiled--a gentle toothless smile.

I became very fond of Salamaweit, as we spent a great deal of time together over several months, working to raise money for showers and toilets for the girls now attending Haile Selassie University. Through the emperor's good graces, a different movie was shown every night at the Palace and, at the request of his grandaughter Seble, we were loaned a copy of The Lion in Winter. "I'll see if the movie theater people will loan us their movie house for a night, and if we can sell enough tickets, we might make a lot of money." Salamaweit was hopeful. We had the tickets printed and then, for days, we drove all over Addis to every conceivable business office, no matter how small and coaxed and harassed until we had sold all our tickets. It was a truly gala night. Salamaweit made a speech, and I made one too.

4.

Ō

Our Children Enroll in the British School

By the 1960s, the size of the United States military presence in Ethiopia necessitated the building of a grade school and high school in Addis Ababa, and all the teachers were American. "Why, John? Why are we Americans so afraid of exposing our kids to other cultures?" Most of the military lived in what was known as the "American Compound" near the Army base, and they shopped at an Army commissary. One night John and I were invited for dinner at an officer's home. As the wife served she beamed proudly, "Everything on the table is from the United States, even the ice cream we're having!"

The American grade school and high school buildings were cookie cutter copies of schools in Palo Alto, California, or in Omaha, Nebraska. What was worse, the high school had admitted exactly nine token Ethiopians.

On the other hand the student body at the British School, housed in a collection of rather tumbledown buildings, was half Ethiopian and the other half included students from forty-two countries. And yes, they would accept our two teenagers.

After the first week of school, Wendy asked, "Mom, are Yugoslavs communists?"

"Well, yes, darling. The country is communist right now. Why?"

"My best friends are twins, a boy and a girl, and they are from Yugoslavia." Goodbye provincialism!

What a marvel the British School was for our California-educated children, who had attended schools in Menlo Park--where the school system went from one grade school for the district (when my older children attended) to seven grade schools by the time Wendy and Robert enrolled. It was a crazy time in California, which had to try and cope with an influx of 10,000 people a day. The first week of school, Robert's English teacher from Great Britain hurled his composition book at him: "Take it back, and write legibly, with a date and margins." A few weeks later, as we ate our leisurely lunch at home during the British School's two-hour lunch break, Robert commented: "American teachers are just as good as English teachers. They just don't make you do the work."

At thirteen Robert was beginning to lose his little boy chubbiness, if not the freckles on his nose. His hair was light brown and hung nearly to his collar. The British School soon insisted on a somewhat shorter haircut.

"What are you tucking in your trousers, Robert, besides your shirttail?"

"A book, Mother. Mr. Kassman might decide to paddle me. He often paddles students."

"Oh, Robert!" Fifteen-year-old sister Wendy was not buying the paddling bit. "Gaby has been at the English School for years and he was never paddled."

"That's because Gaby is from an important family, and he speaks about seven languages and can get himself out of anything."

Gabriel, or Gaby, was Wendy's new boy friend. Wendy was a gorgeous nubile bud, with mops of golden-brown curls, chocolate brown eyes, and her sunny disposition drew boys like a magnet.

"I'm glad I'm going with Gaby, because the other boys leave me alone!"

Gaby Behesnilian was third-generation Armenian in Ethiopia and was raised by his father, as his mother died shortly after the birth of her only child. Mrs. Behesnilian had desperately wanted a child, but had no luck until one night, we were told, when "an angel visited me and said I would have a baby boy." Her fine son arrived, but the angel came and took the mother. Gaby's grandfather had come to Addis Ababa in the 1930s as an economic advisor to Haile Selassie. Gaby's father was born on the farm, where he still lived near the town of Debra Zete, south of Addis. There he had a large flourmill and raised hogs as well--they ate the chaf from the milled wheat. Our family benefited from Wendy's romance, as we were often invited for Sunday lunch at the Behesnilian farm. The long, food-laden table was stately, stood on the vast lawn, the piece de resistance, a roasted suckling pig that always arrived at the table with a fresh rose in its mouth. One Sunday after the main course, Robert turned to Mr. Behesnialian asking, "May I please be excused?" "No." said Gaby's father. Just no. Robert's eyes widened but he stayed put.

I loved talking with Gaby because his sentences were interspersed with words from one of his many languages. If a word sounded better in French (grade

33

school education), or Italian (his nanny), or Amharic (the servants), or Armenian (his native tongue) Gaby would simply lift that word. Frequently his multilingual sentences would include, "OK. OK."

Gaby drove a Mercedes station wagon. In those days no such model existed before but Emperor Haile Selassie had ordered one specially made for him and then did not like it, so Mr. Behesnilian bought it for Gaby. "The car is heavy and safe. Its good for Gaby, who has to make the 30-mile drive from Debra Zete north to Addis every day."

Before Gaby's senior year at the British School ended, his father died. John and I took Robert and Wendy to Debra Zete for the funeral, which was delayed several days, as Gaby waited for his uncle, a priest from Venice, to arrive. The day of the burial we mourners fasted until late afternoon and then gathered at the farm as servants and farm field workers came to pay their respects--a crowd of at least 200. Gaby told them they could perform their dances around the coffin. Later, that sturdy young boy, Gaby, now fatherless as well as motherless, spoke to all the workers, thanking them for their faithfulness, their work, and their presence. After the internment, during the feast, John and I wondered at Gaby's poise. "I just want to put my arms around him and hug." "No, Mimi, I believe he is too fragile just now." But I did open my arms and he came into them, sobbing. Gradually he quieted and we all ate, after a long, tragic day. Later, Gaby would come to the United States and get his university degree from the University of Southern California.

The British School put on an athletic day twice a year. Wendy represented our family honor as one of the runners in the relay race. All around the perimeter of the school racetrack, the teachers had placed furniture, old couches, straight-backed chairs, armchairs, and stools for the comfort of the parents and visitors. Part way through the events we were all invited in for libations-- including scotch, to John's delight. "I'll lay you a bet, Mimi, that at the American school graduation they drink lemonade!"

The British colony in Addis Ababa had a number of fund-raising events each year. Sometimes it would be a play or musical with the teachers playing all parts. We greatly looked forward to these occasions as a welcome change from the Saturday night old western movies at the only movie theater in town. John and I were as yet unfamiliar with the British style--outwardly formal, but at a party, wild! At our first British School party, a pot-luck supper with all the women in evening dresses, one father got so drunk that he passed out on the floor in front of the bar. Another man stood sipping his own drink with his foot resting on the chest of his passed out friend.

The next year's potluck supper was even more exotic--a real ball. On that memorable night, Mr. Casbon, the children's ruddy headmaster at the British School, stepped to the microphone and beamed, "A case of scotch to the lady whose lingerie reaches me first!" In a flash, the air was filled with flying bras, slips, stockings, and panties. As I was struggling to get my hose off, Mr. Casbon, grinning lasciviously, simply disappeared under silk and nylon. Perhaps it was the British who inspired John and me to give some exotic parties as we began to feel "at home" in Addis Ababa.

5 &

An Ancient Christian Kingdom

Ethiopia? Where is Ethiopia? The summer of 1969, John and I made our first trip back to the United States from our Ford Foundation assignment in East Africa. We found that at least half the people we encountered had not heard of Ethiopia--in spite of Haile Selassie's famous speech before the League of Nations in the 1930s. "Maybe it has always been so, John. I certainly never heard of Ethiopia when I was growing up." Indeed, no epigraphic mention of Ethiopia is found in Greek or Latin sources until the second century A.D., when Ptolemy refers to Axum as "the location where the palace of the king is located."

As John and I began to explore the countryside around Addis Ababa, we found ourselves becoming ever more intrigued by the unique history of our highland plateau home. Our sleep was disrupted almost every morning at three by the chanting in our neighborhood Coptic church, a constant reminder of the importance of Christianity to the Amhars since the middle of the fourth century A.D.

Homer wrote in the eighth century B.C., in The Odyssey, "of the distant Ethiopians, the furthest outpost of mankind...."

Herodotus, in his writings more than 400 years before Christ, clearly identifies Ethiopia with Nubia. An anonymous second-century account of travel and trade talks about "the city of the people called Axumites."

The Axum stellas

Ptolemy, the great Egyptian astronomer of the first half of the second century A.D. discusses Ethiopia, and in the sixth century Cosmas Indiccopleustes (writing about Christian Topography) visited the kingdom of Axum.

The kingdom of Axum was the third country in the world to mint coins, the other two being Rome and Persia. Indeed, it is because of their coinage that historians know the name of every emperor of Axum, since each one saw to it that his image and name were placed on the coins he had authorized.

Diodorus, a historian of the first century A.D. wrote; "The Ethiopians say that the Egyptians are one of their colonies which was brought into Egypt by Osiris. The Ethiopians allege that this colony was originally under water, but that the Nile, dragging much mud as it flowed from Ethiopia, had finally filled in and made it part of the continent... They add that from them [the Ethiopians] as from their authors and ancestors, the Egyptians get most of their laws. It is from them that the Egyptians have learned to honor kings as gods...sculpture and writing were invented by the Ethiopians."

In the tenth century A.D., a female enters the political scene. "Regarding the land of Abyssinia it has been governed for years by a woman." She killed the Abyssinia king and took over. Some historians say she was the queen of the Falashas and a daughter of their chief, Gideon. Others claim she was the daughter of King Delnaad, the last Axumite, and that she married the king of the new Zague dynasty whose line would produce King Lalibela. From then to the close of the middle Ages, Ethiopia was generally removed from the view of the outside world, existing in an isolation that was tumultuous rather than splendid.

The image of Ethiopia was transformed by conversion to Christianity early in the fourth century. Two Greek-speaking Christian youths from Syria were shipwrecked off the Red Sea coast and were brought to

Axum. There the king appointed one of them as royal scribe and treasurer. The other spent his time converting people of the noble families to Christianity. Later, the patriarch of Alexandria appointed that young man to be the first bishop of Ethiopia.

Ethiopia possesses the ancient powerful Tabernacle of the Law and the Chariot, The Ark of the Covenant (the tablets of law God gave to Moses on Mt. Siani). Its presence in Ethiopia is explained through the events surrounding Menelik, the son of Solomon and Sheba (an Ethiopian), who returned to Jerusalem to be anointed by his father as King of Ethiopia. Solomon sent the sons of the leading families of Israel to accompany the boy, but fearing that he might spend the rest of his life in a remote part of the world and never see the Ark again, he carried the Ark of the Covenant away with him across the Red Sea to Axum.

Long before the Christian era in Ethiopia, Semites, who, by the time of the conquest, had been converted to Judaism, conquered one of the Hamite groups. The mixture of Hamite and Semite produced the language called Ge'ez and a flourishing empire whose seat was at Axum, a town in the province of Tigre in northern Ethiopia. In its day the splendor and sophistication of the kingdom of Axum rivaled that of ancient Rome. Axum is the Rome of Ethiopia, and the Ge'ez language comparable to Latin in modern Europe. Even today Ge'ez remains the language of the Ethiopian Christian Church.

Axum's light began to dim in the seventh century A.D., and that had much to do with the advance of the belligerent forces of Islam and the encroachment of Abyssinian Christianity. The early centuries of Islam exercised full control of sea borne trade of the Red Sea, and this increased Ethopian isolation as it fought to protect its Christian heritage. The Muslim merchants pushed ever onward in pursuit of merchandise for commerce. The word neggadice in Amharic, means "merchant", yet to the Galla peoples of southern Ethiopia the word simply means "Muslim".

The Muslims living in the southern part of the country built a huge commercial market in a product called kat in Arabic and chat in Amharic. We first learned of chat when son Robert came home one day from the market, "I saw these guys lying on big sacks full of a dried leaves. Yeardow says those leaves are called chat and that lots of poor people chew the leaves, and it makes them happy." Chat--*catha edulis*--is a shrub whose leaves have a slight stimulating effect and, we learned, chat or kat is widely used by the Ethiopian Muslims.

The Abyssinians lived many years practically removed from the rest of the world, in order to protect their Christianity. Contact between Europe and Ethiopia was re-established when the Portuguese helped Ethiopia repel the Muslims in the sixteenth century. The Muslim challenge to the Christian empire was successfully met, and the Portuguese contributed to the education of the people; yet, because they tried to convert the people to Catholicism, the Portuguese were finally driven from the country in 1633. The Ethiopian monarchs' experience with Catholics planted a deep-seated suspicion of Europeans and threw the country back into an isolation that lasted for centuries, though a few explorers and adventurers braved the remote country.

Scottish explorer James Bruce (born 1730) spent years recording his travels in Africa--including Abyssinia. With Bruce the "classical age" of African discovery opened. Over the next century a number of explorers came and went to Abyssinia's highland stronghold, and in 1854 Sir Richard Burton reached Harrar on "a journey of terrible hazards and epic courage." He was the first European to reach that mysterious city. During the nineteenth century a number of world-famous scholars wrote about Ethiopia--often from information supplied by other men who had explored the field. Many famous names could be cited to bear witness to the abiding fascination that Ethiopian studies have exerted on Europeans of many nations over a long period.

Beside the often-present Muslim threat, the Ethiopians had two serious bouts with the Italians. The first began in 1886 and ended in 1896. By defeating the Italians in 1896, Ethiopia had become the touchstone of the great realignment of world affairs in the 1900s. "Rarely in human history have such vast changes turned on the destiny of a small people struggling to salvage its freedom." In driving out the Italians, King Menelek II, heir to Solomon, had worked a greater miracle than he could have dreamed. Menelek II founded the modern capital, Addis Ababa, ("new flower") in 1898. He ordered the construction of a railway that would originate from the coast (which the French built over a 25 year period). One day Menelek ordered his subjects throughout the land to plant eucalyptus trees in large numbers. The emperor had seen a grove of these trees growing in the British legation gardens. He ordered hundreds of thousands of seedlings, and the tree, quick growing and commercially valuable, has the great propensity of immediately shooting up from its roots when it is cut down. Today Ethiopia is blanketed with eucalyptus trees. When John and I lived in Addis, planting was still going on in a most interesting form. Any adult Ethiopian who enrolled in literacy classes, received 1,000 eucalyptus seedlings to plant. Given the trees growth and many uses (building material, leaves for cooking fires), the citizen could earn a fine cash crop as well as the ability to read!

The Ethiopians' second bout with the Italians occurred in late 1936, when Mussolini invaded the country. He was driven out by the British in 1940-41.

And here I am, writing about our adventures in the highlands of East Africa but I write with no scholarly bent. I write from fascination, admiration, and a deep sense of our fortune in having spent a few years in such a historic country. A unique country from the standpoint of topography, religion, culture, and certainly from the complex mixture of races that have blended over the centuries. In the 1960s and 70s, Ethiopia was the only surviving independent state of Africa. Of all the countries of Africa, Ethiopia alone had an unbroken continuity that stems from the nebulous eras of the Old Testament that give a coherence other African nations lack.

No matter what the rest of the world believes, Ethiopians lay claim to an uninterrupted line of kings descended from Menelik I, the son of King Solomon and the Queen of Sheba. This claim is deeply rooted in Ethiopia and must be considered one of the most powerful and influential national sagas anywhere in the world.

"The imperial dignity shall remain perpetually attached... to the line which descends without interruption from...the Queen of Sheba and King Solomon of Jerusalem." This sentence is part of the 1955 Constitution of Ethiopia, and in a culture where art counts heavily and where painters abound, it is a favorite theme. John and I attended the opening of the Addis Ababa Hilton in 1969 (it had taken eight years to build, much to the frustration of the international Hilton management and the architect--a friend of John's from Cornell.) Along one wall of the Hilton were an Ethiopian artist's stained glass portrayals of the Queen of Sheba and King Solomon legend. That night at the

Hilton the emperor sat on a long raised dais. His son sat several yards to his left--too far away to talk, and his advisor sat the same distance to the right. "It doesn't seem fair, John. He looks so lonesome. So dignified, so remote as his country has been".

"Never forget," John answered, "he is the King of Kings, the Lion of Judah, with all that implies and the descendant of the Queen of Sheba." John shook his head as he tried to reconcile the history of Haile Selassie's family with the Hilton Hotel. All the way home we talked of how the wild and rugged mountains of Ethiopia were great natural obstacles between the various regions of the country. "And I am sure," said John, "that over the centuries those mountain ranges contributed to the marked ethnic, linguistic, and religious diversity of this amazing country."

While Ethiopia cultivated, then preserved the ancient Christian religion, it is also the place where Judaism survived. John and I visited the Jewish villages in the highlands of Ethiopia. Although the highland villages looked exactly like the others in the rest of the country, there would be a synagogue instead of a church. These people are called the Falashas. Quite dark skinned and fine featured, this group of perhaps 60,000 tranquilly practiced their Jewish faith for several thousand years, unconquered by the Muslims, undisturbed by the Christians. They are the only Jews in the world whose ancestors were not touched by the Diaspora. John and I bought a number of the clay and mud figures that the Falashas make to sell to visitors who come to their village. It is said that a Swedish ambassador's daughter came from Addis and taught the Falashas how to fire their statues. (In recent years these people have moved to Israel).

Axum's stele continues to intrigue scholars. Not much is known about the cult they represent, but the people of Ethiopia continue to look to Axum as their holy city. The imperial regalia are kept there and the emperors are crowned on an ancient, crude stone seat in the shadow of the tallest stele. I loved walking among the stele, some as high as 60 feet, while the great majority are 10 to 20 feet. Some are carved with a new moon or the sun, and stele from later dates have a cross hewn into the stone. A virtual forest of monuments. And as I walked I contemplated the centuries and how the word "Coptic" came into being. It emerged after a big theological debate over whether God (as in the Trinity) is really three persons, or whether Christ was wholly divine. Egypt and Ethiopia chose the latter interpretation and their form of Christianity became known as "Coptic," which some say is a European corruption of the word "Egyptic". The Ethiopians do not like the word Coptic to denote their religion, preferring instead Ethiopian Orthodox Church.

Intermarriage has long been a means of solidifying the national elite of Ethiopia. Many medieval Amhara kings took wives from the daughters of Muslim and pagan kings, usually after the baptism of the intended. Haile Selassie married the daughter of a Muslim-born Galla king from Wollo. John and I got to know the children of that marriage, and in each case their mates, and those of Haile Selassie's grandchildren, had also been chosen for them and from another tribe. Indeed, one of Haile Selassie's daughters is still alive and living in Washington D. C. She lives with her daughter Seble (whose husband was Galla), who bore six children. When John and I first knew Seble she headed the crafts school in Addis Ababa, which she had founded. Her sister Ruth built the Seven Olives Hotel in Lalibela, a hotel that would loom large in my life during our second year in Ethiopia.

6 Ƶ

Daily Life in Addis Ababa

I had a terrific toothache, so John's secretary called her
dentist Noe Yancovich. "Tell Mrs. Summerskill to come
in this evening, say after six." When I arrived a lady in
white opened the door, looked at me suspiciously and
demanded: "Min d'nau? What is it?" I pointed to my jaw
and my watch simultaneously, and she somehow
decided I was legitimate. She admitted me to a Tower of
Babel.

Dr. Yancovich's waiting room was crammed with
moaning, reading, yawning, staring people of all
nationalities. Two minutes after I entered the office, a
patient shot out of the treatment room and on out the
front door. Running right behind him was a tall man in
a white coat who stopped short of the exit, pivoted into
a room marked "Laboratory," and reappeared
immediately with a half-smoked cigarette. It was

obviously Noe Yancovich. He called out "Kalispera" to a waiting Greek, "bon soir" to a Frenchman, "tenastilling" to a couple of Ethiopians, and asked me to "please wait." He swooped up the next patient; a gentle looking lady of unknown nationality, and we all heard the drill start immediately as everybody in the waiting room moved up one place.

John had gotten to know Dr. Yancovich well because of accumulated dental problems that required three root canal jobs--with no anesthetic. The doctor's technique was not at all primitive. He was about thirty-five years of age and had been trained in Paris. He had bought the finest equipment, however, when he came to Addis Ababa in the sixties, he found there was only one other dentist with modern training in a city of nearly a million. Since his arrival Dr. Yancovich had been averaging forty-five patients a day! He simply had no time for anesthetics and you were in and out of his chair so fast you did not care.

But the waiting was insufferable. Like other dentists Dr. Yancovich jammed in extra patients with acute pain, and high government officials, ambassadors, and the like were forever claiming priority. One day, when John and I had been there for about an hour and a half, Yancovich strode into the center of his teeming clientele and shouted simultaneous translations of what was meant to be a joke: "I am taking this poor fellow next because he is the father of four children." Immediately mothers and fathers with more than four children screamed back, "I have six!" "I have five!" "I have seven!" I burst out laughing when my husband leapt to his feet and shouted at the retreating dentist's back, "I have eight--do you hear, eight!"

The patient flow in Dr. Yancovich's office was also disrupted by suffering, grieving families. Once, as I entered the small treatment room, five people--two women and three children--were sobbing their way out. I looked at the harassed dentist: "How did you treat them all in here at once?" "I didn't", he said. "There was only one patient. They are Slavs, and the others came to hold hands around the chair and to cry."

Dr. Yancovich, a citizen of Israel, was born in Rumania. He was fluent in six languages, and that was fortunate, because he had to communicate with his Ethiopian dental assistant in Italian, his lab chief and bookkeeper in German, and so on. He was running an international business with at least eight on staff while he spawned another business out on the street: car watching for patients.

The municipality of Addis Ababa had lined Haile Selassie I Avenue with parking meters, and there were plenty of police lounging around waiting for meters to expire. A large corps of street boys also waited around and hustled everyone who drove up as they offered protection against parking tickets. When you returned to your car the street boy claimed he had deposited five cents in the meter, ten cents, or whatever it was. We never questioned the system as we paid out our change, for we never had a ticket.

I stopped going with John on his all-to-frequent visits to Dr. Yancovich, but eagerly awaited his return to hear the office news. When John returned from his evening visits, I would first hand him a martini--his first anesthetic of the day--and ask, "What's the gossip at Yancovich's today?"

"Well, Petty Whipple was there, in a purple body stocking. She said her freshman class would not go back to the university until the emperor apologized, and I said 'For Christ's sake!' Then Bob Yost came in, and I asked why the embassy people didn't go to the U.S. dentists in Aswara and leave more room for us at Yancovich's. He said he preferred Yancovich. I also talked with His

49

Excellency, Yilma Aeressa. Did you know he has a son at Hayward State? And Woijero Edjiguan was there, the one with the beautiful eyes. She looks pregnant again. How dull dental life will seem when we return to America!" My husband sighed, " But then again, I wish we could have the dull driving of America transported to Addis!"

Driving in Ethiopia was really awful. Except for the elite, nearly everyone was a neophyte and there were crashes all the time. The traffic circles in Addis were strewn with glass, cursing drivers, police officers writing accident reports. These police officers were on foot, and one day John was stopped on a circle, by a policeman who ordered him to sit on the right side of the car while driving. John was sitting behind the wheel in his American car, which, of course, had the steering wheel on the left. The policeman was used to British cars, and everyone driving on the left-hand side of the road--as in Britain. In the end John put his bottom on the right-hand seat, and steered himself by leaning to the left until out of the policeman's sight.

Now and then, rounding a corner in Addis Ababa, one was startled by a vehicle that had just assumed some grotesque position on top of a wall, or deep in a gully. Traffic in Ethiopia was compounded by pedestrians and animals alike sharing the roads with the trucks and cars. In Ethiopia, one learns to drive, one hand on the horn, skirting citizens and domestic animals by inches or fractions thereof. Knowing the road habits of the animal species was crucial. Thus, cows that start across a road continue to do so. Sheep run if you blow the horn. Goats, grazing by the roadside, continue grazing. And so on.

Unhappily, there were exceptions to these rules of the road. One night John and I encountered a goat, some sort of genetic deviant, who leapt from a grazing herd directly into our headlights. We had to drive fifty miles back to Addis Ababa without lights, taking to a ditch every time a car or truck came thundering towards us from the opposite direction.

There are three categories of drivers in Ethiopia. First, there are government officials, businessmen, etc., who drive their own Mercedes, desperately attempting to keep them undented. Second, there are professional drivers who keep their jobs with embassies and corporations based on amazing reflex skills and great good luck. Then there is everyone else.

Everyone else charges ahead with traditional pride and independence in lieu of driving experience. Auto repair shops in Addis were living monuments to the fierce Ethiopian individualism that brought the Italians to their knees at the Battle of Adowa.

Running as we did from the problems at San Francisco State University, John and I had neglected to obtain our international driving licenses. I had let my California permit run out, and John had lost his wallet (drivers license enclosed), and we launched ourselves to take the long, rigorous examinations for an Ethiopian driving license. Sheer boredom and time wasting it seemed, though we have had pleasure since in presenting our licenses, all in Amharic, to Hertz car people in Paris, New York, and other unlikely places.

Yeardow drove us to the licensing bureau, where we joined a very long line to get an equally long application form. "John, why do you suppose all these Ethiopian men are lounging about?" We soon found out as one stepped forward and offered, for a modest fee, to complete our application in Amharic. Like fortunetellers, those men could answer every question, even date of birth, by one quick glance at each of us.

Next we had to seek certification that we were physically able to drive. At the government hospital, crowded with sick people, an Italian physician carefully measured my blood pressure, then John's and, after paying the fee, we were given certificate number one.

Next came our hearing exam. The Yugoslav doctor, dressed in green surgical gown and cap, approached us with an enormous tuning fork. With some anxiety we watched him motion each patient to sit before what looked like a giant anvil. The doctor called for silence, raised the great fork above his head, and struck the anvil with the strength of a blacksmith. We saw patients lifted from their chairs by the clash, nevertheless, upon payment of the fee, we received certificate number two, "hearing good." We progressed on to an elaborate eye exam, and into a room where aspirants had to be able to read all the international driving signs, and where a man asked, in Amharic, questions about Ethiopian motor laws, the proper operation of vehicles, etc. He switched to English when he got to John and me, but his comment to each hopeful driver: "Miss two questions and you are out!" was the same for everyone.

Finally in possession of all necessary certificates, we proceeded to the man who would accompany us in our car while we proved we could drive. "How long have you been driving?" he asked John. When John said, twenty-five years, he exploded, "Then why are you taking the test?! No foreigners take this test. They pay someone to take it for them!"

Mostly people walked. Every day we watched the thousands of men and women who walked along the sides of a road, or crammed themselves into the jitney minibuses. "Everyone is going somewhere, John. From where to where?" Ethiopia has dozens and dozens of holidays. I suppose if one lives in an ancient culture, days of celebration--for one reason or another--build up over the centuries. Many were Christian holidays, celebration days John and I had never heard of, but others were tribal feast days. Perhaps much of the going and coming had to do with those feast and religious days. When the walkers were women we would often see them squatting in a circle on the side of the highway, chatting happily, their lovely sheer white cotton skirts spread around them. "John, Why do you think they sit that way and get their skirts all dirty?" "Mimi! They're peeing. You must have guessed that!" I had not.

7

The Marcado

"Aklilu says the marcado (market place) in Addis is the largest in all of Africa." It was easy to believe John's statement as I had just returned from my weekly foray into the vast fields of the marcado. It is huge! Blocks and blocks of bustle as far as one can see and further than one wants to walk. The indigenous people, and this means at least a million, buy practically everything they eat or wear within the few square miles that encompass the marcado. More important it is perhaps a social center for the people of the country's largest city.

For the visitor, ferengi (foreigner), the market offers endless fascination. The "new market" contains a block of small souks for buying things like crosses, wooden sculptures, daggers, fly whisks made from horses tails, monkey skin rugs, Queen of Sheba cartoon paintings, and baskets, baskets, and baskets, ranging from tiny, round baskets (great for keeping jewelry or bobby pins) to baskets the size of a round dining table. The monkey skin rugs are illegal as they are fashioned from the long silky-haired skins of the colobus monkey that faces extinction. One hopes they are no longer for sale.

Wearing low-heeled shoes, and with my shoulder bag slung across my chest, I always allowed a half-day for our marcado excursion. Yeardow was my companion as we wandered, bargained, and carried things back to the car.

At the far edge of the marcado, the farthest place from downtown Addis is the hairdressing section. Here sit ladies under umbrellas, having their hair braided in a dozen tiny plaits that are then rubbed with rancid butter. This hair-do lasts a good three months or more. It is practical, but sort of smelly. Edjigia never had her hair done in plaits--actually she quite disapproved!

Nearby the hair dressing area is the tin can market. Everyone in Addis saves bottles and cans, and the servants sell them to men from the market that make a living converting them into useful household products. Take, for example, the huge oil drums. The two ends are cut out, and these ends become frying pans, 'Ethiopian style,' their concave surface being exactly right for cooking injera (a pancake-like bread) or for roasting green coffee beans. Small cooking stoves, hibachi-style, are made from the sides of the drum. Small cans, about tuna-fish size, are made into lamps. A top is welded on with a hole and spout put in it. The cans are filled with liquid paraffin (purchased at the local gas station), a cloth wick is inserted, and the family lamp is ready for use. John and I owned many of these tiny lamps and at party time would place them along the stone walls in front of our house and line the paths with their merry flickering to welcome guests.

However, it was the great Addis horse market that created the most interest for the hundreds of people who hung around the marcado. Since time immemorial Ethiopia has been a great country for horses and horsemen. Good horsemanship was an essential for all the noble families, especially for warriors. For centuries at war with Muslim neighbors, the soldiers had to have a fine mount--and a mule. As long ago as the thirteenth century Marco Polo wrote, "The Ethiopians are the best soldiers I have encountered." And certainly the superb horsemanship displayed in the 1896 Battle of Adawa was greatly responsible for the defeat of the Italians, so historians declare!

In the old days a man might well be known by the name of his horse. The warrior would not ride his horse except in battle. A groom would lead the horse outfitted with a fine saddle, colorful blankets, and emblems as well as small, dangling iron stirrup rings. In battle the master, barefooted, would insert his big toe, and perhaps another toe as well, in the stirrup. Most of the time, however, the master rode behind his handsome mount, ambling along on his mule.

The saddle street of the marcado is fascinating, as literally dozens of men and boys are at work, tooling leather, sawing wood, gluing and cutting leather for bridles and halters. Other men fit buckles and the bit onto the bridles and halters, while young boys tie them onto miniature bells and brightly colored pompoms.

Ethiopians do not merely like horses, to own one is a symbol of status. Driving in the countryside on Sundays, John and I enjoyed watching the village men as they rode out. Mostly they walked their horses, while chatting with friends. Sometimes it was a real cowboy scene. A young man would streak by, bent over the neck of his mount in the traditional jockey position. The highland horses are about the size of our quarter horses. The Ethiopian saddle is small by our standards, though western in style, hence has a pommel. The back of the saddle is straighter than ours and rather fan-shaped. My favorite piece of ensemble is the saddle blanket. Usually made of red, purple, or blue velvet, it is about a yard-and-a-half in length and half as wide. The two ends, elaborately embroidered in scrolls and squiggles, form a W. In the center of the squiggles is a lion, machine embroidered in free-style. These lions are popeyed, quizzical, and utterly enchanting!

I had grown up on horseback, so to speak. My father, having been raised on a ranch, bought me a Shetland pony when I was five years old. From then on I always had a horse, which was stabled at Grandfather LaFollette's ranch near Pullman, Washington. At seventeen, I was made queen of the Whitman County Rodeo--much to my embarrassment. However, the $75 prize money helped me weather the three days of sitting in the "queen's box" at the rodeo. So when son Robert, age 13, suggested we get a couple of horses and ride together--I agreed. Once we bought the horses, two only, and installed them in our fancy horse stable, with a horse shower, we went shopping for saddles and the works.

The saddle-shopping venture took us first to the saddle blanket area of the marcado, where dozens and dozens of souks sell fabric of every variety. Many of the fabric souks have a resident tailor who sits in front of the shop, his feet pumping energetically, machine wheel whirring. Addis has several Singer Sewing Machine shops (Mr. Singer did get around!) selling mostly nonelectric machines. Some of the tailors, independent of a shop, could be found in the middle of a field, busily stitching away. Ethiopians by the thousands purchase a piece of cloth and have it made up into a simple dirndl, or trousers or a jacket.

"John, Yeardow and I are going to the marcado today to buy uniforms." A new uniform twice a year is part of the salary paid to a servant--that and one sheep for each servant for every holiday. It always fascinated me to see the hundreds of sheepskins being carried back to the market on the day after any holiday. There they would be sold for rugs, grain sacks, and parchment for pictures or wine skins.

On uniform-buying day the male servants and I got in our station wagon and repaired to a certain souk run by an elderly Ethiopian. He had two helpers –one, his son--for measuring and selling. The sewing machine man always sat at his machine, stitching and listening as Ato Waulie and our two Asafas discussed and argued fabrics and styles. Ato Waukie always selected khaki trousers for day use and white for parties. At all times of day he wore a white doctorlike coat on top. The two Asafas invariably selected khaki for the pants, shirts and jackets, arguing only about the shade and the quality of the Japanese-manufactured fabric. Daba, who took care of the horses, was our individualist. He loved to wear white, aside from the Sunday and holiday whites that all Ethiopians wear, and was particularly fond of white Jodhpur pants. It was a struggle to get him to order khakis for daily use. All the time these clothing debates were going on, the old tailor was measuring and calling out the figures to his son. In the meantime twenty or thirty men would have gathered in the doorway, all offering advice.

Uniform shopping with Edjigia was sheer fun, as she loved choosing bright colored fabrics. Sometimes I would steal away to a nearby shop, where they sold incredibly magnificent umbrellas, gold embroidered on stripes of colored velvet and fringed. These umbrellas were sold to priests, who carry those large protectors on religious holidays and for weddings and funerals.

John had suggested that we look for "some kind of box that we could use for supplies on our camping trips." On one shopping day at the marcado, we discovered wooden trunks and boxes. "Discovered" is a mild word for finding ourselves in the middle of literally thousands of boxes. In every direction as far as we could see, there were shops selling boxes. Made from packing cases, and in every conceivable size, they were painted or stained in brilliant colors. The insides were lined with newspapers, colored Sunday supplements being the paper of choice. The fancier boxes had a fixture for padlocking, and nearby one could buy the padlock from a salesman whose wares dangled on huge rings from various parts of his body.

The marcado also had handsome rugs for sale. Woven of coarse wool in beige, brown, and black, their geometric designs are reminiscent of Navajo Indian rugs. Sometimes a bold-faced lion is woven into the design, his large Coptic eyes staring out at the observer. (It was possible to buy bright-colored rugs as well, but these came from Princess Seble's craft center.) At the rug sellers one could also buy capes. Made of rough, dark brown wool, they have an attached hood, almost identical to the peasant capes of Greece. Along the back of the cape is a long sheathlike piece that serves as a rifle cover.

A great deal of furniture is made in the marcado. Simple wooden chairs, square tables, wardrobes, beds and mattresses, and wicker extras such as baskets, bassinettes, and waste baskets. When an Ethiopian purchased furniture, it would be delivered on the head of a deliveryman--if the purchaser lived nearby. Otherwise the various pieces are piled on top of one of the tiny blue taxis. This scurrying little car is enormously important to the Addis Ababan, for it conveys not only the driver, but also his grain, his bed, or rushes his laboring wife to the hospital. Hordes of these tiny cabs ply the streets that fan out from the main plaza, picking up passengers en route and piling people in--one on top of the other.

There are many gold shops in the marcado. Ethiopian jewelry is finely crafted and the gold is a lovely deep yellow, at least 22 carats. Other marcado shops sold ancient cowhide shields, and there were many souks peddling icons--usually not very old, yet very well crafted. One could endlessly examine scrolls and Coptic paintings and if lucky perhaps make a real "find."

Then, having selected your wares, the fun would begin. Rule number one, never ask a price unless you intend to buy. From then on--anything goes. Bargaining embarrassed me a bit, so I was shy about the whole process. However, I loved being with a good trader and listening to the hype or depreciation of the desired item. It is a marvelous show--the feigned anger at a low offer; the buyer's stalking out the door (well, almost out) and, finally, the smiles and handshakes, the friendship forged during the lengthy exchange. It is the bargaining that adds character to the marcado, giving color and pace to one's days, bringing the believer back again and again.

As in any market, the food section is the most vital and intriguing. There are several blocks in the grain market, and it is here that every housewife comes to examine and taste the grains she will need for her family. Bakers as well as hotelkeepers come to bargain. All day the small brown donkeys, singly and in groups, arrive at the grain market burdened with their master's crop.

Nearby is the sheep market, where men haggled over the price of an animal day in and day out. The red pepper market displayed massive piles of red peppers that were sorted and stuffed into huge gunnysacks. Red pepper forms the base of the berberi powder that is the heart of the Ethiopian meal. It was obvious that we should immediately buy at least one makacha--a hollowed out log with a waistline. The lower part is solid, the upper two-thirds about two feet deep. Into this vessel went the spices that, along with the red peppers, make up berberi. Our servants, using giant-sized wooden pestles, would take turns pulverizing the peppers. Two would work at a time, alternating their blows and often singing. Until then John, the children, and I had eaten only plain old American food. Ato Walkie was very happy the day he could begin to serve us, at least sometimes, food he thought worth eating--hot and spicy.

8

Ethiopian Cuisine

Thump-thump, thump-thump, the rhythm of the pounding pestles created a solemn drum beat. It was impossible to work, so I went out to our back terrace. On the lawn below the veranda the servants and their friends were gathered around the large wooden makacha. Two at a time pounded. Each had a clublike wooden pestle, and up and down, up and down they alternated strokes. We were making berberi. We had gradually acquired five makachas of varied sizes for pounding different products. The coffee beans one was quite small, about ten inches high and eight inches across the center. I had been hollowed out in the middle down to six inches and decorated on the sides with simple carving. We bought the green coffee beans at the market, then roasted them in small batches on a round, concave piece of iron, actually that roasting pan made from the end of an oil drum. The sizes of the berberi-making makacha depend somewhat on the size of the tree from which they are hollowed. All makachas we bought now sit on the porch of my log house in New Jersey, un-used but not unloved.

Ethiopian food consists essentially of injera and wot. Injera is a bread and rather like a huge buckwheat pancake cooked on one side only. Wot is the sauce traditionally eaten with injera and it comes in many forms. Doro wot (chicken), berg wot (lamb), and kilt wot (dried peas) are the most common. The base of the sauce is berberi.

Our family liked wot, so occasionally I would buy a small sack of berberi from the grocers. When our Ethiopian friends discovered that we bought berberi they were scandalized.

"No, you must make your own."

"How do you know who made it, or what they put in it? How do we start?"

They stared in disbelief. How could I have lived months in Addis Ababa and not understand. "Your servants will know. Ask Edjigia."

"How much shall we make? How much do you make at a time?"

"Oh, enough for six months at least--or a year," came the nonchalant answer.

The servants were excited and pleased that the ferenges were to have their own berberi. That very afternoon Yeardow took Edjigia and me to the marcado to buy supplies. Proper, formal, and speaking precise English, Yeardow did not fit in with the other servants. For Yeardow, driving was the highest of callings, and his navy blue uniform and cap set him apart as well. We drove in our Volkswagen while once again he complained, "Madame, why don't we buy a Mercedes?

It is a fine car and more fitting." He drove us slowly up the rough rock street to the spice market. Suddenly Edjigia saw red peppers she liked, and after endless sampling and bargaining we hoisted the mammoth gunnysack of red peppers into the car--a sack at least five feet tall. At home Edjigia dumped the peppers out on the back lawn to sort them. "Mama, mama," she called, "peppers no good, too many seeds." So back they went into their sack, and we started the whole process over again. The merchant was not at all perturbed when we returned the peppers. He immediately produced another sack that was to Edjigia's liking. She was all smiles.

Beautiful, beautiful Edjigia was the delight of the compound. Some days her hair was worn pulled back and high, Egyptian-style, but more often she wore a bright scarf around her piled up hair. Now and then she would plait her hair into two fat braids that stuck out saucily. For the next three weeks she was the most important person in the compound, as she was the boss of the berberi. Three weeks—for that's how long it took to make our berberi.

Peppers seeded, the pounding process began and continued for several hours a day (until everyone was sneezy and watery-eyed and all the peppers were reduced to coarse flakes. The various servants, their friends and relatives, came to watch and to take their turn at pounding. Asafa, the night guard, brought his tiny daughter down from their cottage. Roly-poly Ababa (flower) danced around the makacha in delight, her wisp of a dress so short it exposed her round and naked bottom.

The pepper flakes were now placed in the sun to dry--on an old bedspread I had resurrected. Each night they were brought inside in case of rain. Finally one day

Edjigia announced that the peppers were properly dry. "Now, mama, we go marcado again to buy spices." I followed her as she raced from spice lady to spice lady and her critical eye searched out the best of each spice. In the end we had eleven bundles wrapped in newspapers, containing everything but the needed garlic which we grew that ourselves.

All the spices were added to the peppers, and the pounding began once again. The coarse substance was then moistened and allowed to sit, well covered, for the day in order to blend well. Then it was taken up to Edjigia's wot bet (kitchen). Ethiopians often have their kitchen separate from the rest of the house. It is usually a small square building fashioned of eucalyptus poles, mud, and dung. The walls do not meet the thatched roof, resulting in a smoke-escape hatch that sort of works. She had the fire going on her small hibachilike stove, burning tiny pieces of eucalyptus wood, bark, and leaves. "Why do you have two piles of peppers?" I asked. "See, mama, one pile is coarser than the other, and the little ones will cook faster."

It took hours and hours to roast batch after batch on top of the oil drum pan John had dubbed that "flying saucer," but we were now ready to go to the mill.

Piling into the station wagon with our two huge plastic bags of unground berberi, we drove a short distance over the rough road to the neighborhood mill. Addis has many of these small rocky roads made from rectangles of hewn stone. Because of heavy rains all roads must be hard surfaced, but the rock-made ones were exceedingly bumpy and death on tires. We got in line with a number of Ethiopians waiting to grind their berberi, corn, or grain. When our turn came nearly everyone put something over his or her face as the

66

primitive grinder roared into action. The air was soon powdery pink, and I was glad when the precious beriberi, now ready for use, was back in its plastic bags.

Nearly three weeks had passed. We were almost in business. "Now we make injera." In Edjigia's kitchen we took her "starter" (just as in making sourdough bread), made from a fine grain called tef, and poured in water until about pancakelike consistency. She then poured the dough in a circular stream that curled like a fourth of July pinwheel. She poured so evenly, and when the bubbles appeared in the injera, she did not flip it over, but put a convex lid over it. Soon the first perfectly round injera was ready. When we had a goodly stack, Edjigia put the starter away for next time.

Meanwhile, we could hear cackling and commotion, as Ato Walkie and Asafa chased and killed two of our chickens. The cleaned chickens were cut, each into eleven pieces in a manner completely strange to my way of chicken cutting. As these pieces boiled, Ato Walkie browned onions, adding berberi, the chicken stock, and salt and pepper. After boiling for about two hours, sometimes adding a little stock, the chicken pieces were combined with the mixture, and finally several whole hard-boiled eggs. We ate injera by tearing big rounds into long strips, rolling them up like a jelly roll and putting them on our plates along with some pieces of chicken, an egg and some sauce. A torn off piece of injera was used to pick up the wot. Forks and knives would have been strangely inappropriate.

Sometimes we ate our native food at our own dining room table, but other days we ate on our porch sitting at the round woven basket table that Ethiopians used. The table, designed in colorful geometric patters, stood at approximately 30 inches. But first Edjigia would arrive with a pitcher of warm water and basin. We each washed our hands, before and after the meal. Each person would have a round injera and a pile of wot. Tearing off a piece of the injera, we would again use it to pick up the wot. "John, I sometimes get the feeling I am tearing up a piece of table cloth and using it to eat!"

We did not ever make tela (beer) ourselves, but the servants always did for a holiday—and, as mentioned, there are many! Usually Ato Walkie would arrive with a bundle of leaves from a medium-sized bush called gecho. These were dried and crushed, and later wheat, barley, and tef all came in contact with the gecho leaves. This grayish-green beer would finally be strained, often through gauze, and put in old whisky bottles. That is why all old bottles are a treasure! At Mescal, we were always given several bottles of gecho tela. On our second Mescal holiday our servants built their own private Mescal tower of wood, copying the huge one built downtown for the emperor. Their's was at least twenty feet in height, the servants and families danced and sang around its flames in between drinking homemade tela. John and I watched, celebrating by drinking scotch whisky.

We did make our own tege. It is a delicious wine made from honey and the leaves of the gecho bush. We boiled the leaves and then added honey to the brew, which was then poured into a mammoth jug and sealed with clay. Every few days Edjigia would break the seal, add more honey, and reseal. Orange peel tied in a cloth was immersed into the liquid for a better color. A month later we were allowed our first sip. At that stage the drink is cloudy and called beurz, but was delicious. Later it clears into a rich golden color. We liked tege and often served it at dinner parties instead of the good, but uninspiring, Ethiopian wine.

Then, of course, there is the fabulous Ethiopian coffee. While espresso is served in most bars, in their homes Ethiopians made a ritual of coffee making, brewing and rebrewing. In order to have really fresh coffee, our family has always had coffee beans, home ground in a strong cast iron grinder that we bought decades ago in England. In Addis, however, we went a step further as we bought green coffee beans. Living in the country where coffee originated forces you to pay special attention. Having carefully selected the green beans in the marcado, at home Edjigia would sort through them for any bad ones. Then the concave, platterlike oil drum top used for injera and berberi was placed over the gas burner on our stove and beans poured onto it, no oil, no anything, just heat. For a long, long time Edjigia or Ata Walkie would stand by, a metal poker stick in hand to keep the beans constantly moving. When they had turned the proper shade of brown (in our case a deep chocolate color) they were removed. All this while the delicious odor or roasting coffee permeated every room of the house.

Since the ceilings in our house were of canvas stretched over a skeleton wooden frame, the sound of the coffee grinder became an alarm clock for John and me. We could hear the soft clink of silver and china as Edjigia set the breakfast table on the porch off our bedroom. Soon we would be drinking juice from freshly-squeezed oranges and eating eggs that our chickens had laid. We would then devour sourdough toasted bread that Ato Walkie made from a starter I had bought from a small Left Bank Parisian bakery and moved from

69

refrigerator to refrigerator on the long journey to Paris to Addis.

So Addis gradually became home for us, perhaps partly because we baked our own bread, built the chicken coop for our egg-laying chickens, and grew our own fabulous vegetable garden. We even had an artichoke plant, and our sweetcorn sometimes boasted more than a few kernels. So with coffee roasting, tege brewing, and the long but friendly process of making berberi we knew we were fortunate, living a good and very real life.

9   𝕌

The Challenge Giving Creative Parties

"Romeo and Juliet? Mother, you must be kidding!"

We were planning a big party for Ethiopian friends, and I announced to my family, "This time I am not going to have all the Ethiopian men sitting and talking along one side of the living room and all the Ethiopian women huddled along the other side. "Everyone will have a name pinned to their back, one of the names of some famous couple. Like Romeo and Juliet. Whoever has the name Solomon will have to go find Sheba and so on. Then they are to escort their partner to dinner."

Our children refused to have anything to do with this impending disaster. The whole notion was hard for them to accept.

"To kill all those chickens just because they are roosters."

"But, darlings, we now have 12 hens and we don't want to feed 20 roosters as well. We don't need them!"

The chicken episode had amused our servants enormously. We were buying eggs from the marcado, and about every second egg we cracked in our kitchen had been fertilized, and so we had to throw them away. "I have an idea, John. Why don't we buy our own chickens, hens this time? We will finally have our own eggs."

"If we get our own chickens, we'd better build a chicken coop first," my sensible John advised. He and Robert had already rewired our whole house and felt up to any task. So one Sunday morning, after the family game of croquet, they began construction on our chicken coop. The theory was that the hens should be high off the ground because of predators. Hyenas, the "garbage collectors" of Addis Ababa, ran nightly through our streets. Also there were small wildcats in the neighborhood and God knows what else. Neighbors had told us to stay in our car if it broke down when returning from a party at night.

"It is because of the shiftas (bandits), and wild animals." We had noticed that these servants who lived outside the compound, never walked after dark. By Sunday evening we proudly stood back to admire our chicken run, which was about thirty square feet and had twenty little wood cubicles wire fronts. These were perched up about three feet above the ground on a frame of poles. Daytime Asafa, John, and Robert were rightly proud of their handiwork.

The next week John and I drove down to the agricultural division of Haile Selassie University, which was located in Dire Dawa. There, consulting with the manager of the farm, we purchased twenty white-with-red-topnotch chickens. Every day they would run about their pen, and at dusk Robert and a couple of servants would catch each chicken, amid much screeching and squawking, and place the cackling bird in one of the cubicles. But no eggs were forthcoming. "Maybe the trauma of moving is responsible." I suggested. "Ah," said the agricultural professors, " it is traumatic to move chickens. Give them time." We gave them time--still no eggs.

Then one day we had an illustrious guest for lunch. Bethal Webster was a trustee of the Ford Foundation (John's employer) and, though a prominent New York lawyer, Mr. Webster had been born and raised on a Colorado farm. After lunch, and with some pride, John escorted everyone out to see the chicken run with its twenty tiny roosts. "Splendid, splendid," said Mr. Webster and then blasted, "Why in the hell do you have twenty roosters? You'll never get any eggs!" A farm lady from Sweden who had long lived in Addis sold us good, healthy hens, and the roosters made marvelous chicken salad for our dinner party.

So the night of the party arrived. Even John was leery of my name-pinning idea and sulked in a corner, drinking martinis with a couple of Ethiopian cronies. As guests arrived, Edjigia helped me pin a name on each person's back. Curiosity got everyone's attention when I explained the idea of the game. Immediately, I noticed some of the Ethie men getting ready, prowling, looking over the field. Then I said, "Ready, set, go!" It was a madhouse--men racing across the room, spinning women to see their name tags, pushing people aside to get at their partners. John dissolved in laughter and delighted in his Juliet. Reluctantly we bid our guests goodnight. You know when you have given a really good party. Our family was feeling happy (and some of us even high), and we were giggling with the staff when suddenly John appeared holding a bottle of soda water spray and squirting each of us in turn. Edjigia hid outside, I climbed in a cupboard. Soon the squeals died down and we all crept out to find that John had disappeared. Perhaps he'd gone for a walk in the compound? I shooed Wendy and Robert off to bed when suddenly there was an infuriated scream from Robert. As he had begun to get into bed, John had shot out from under the covers, a white napkin tied around his face like a bandit, giving Robert a long cold squirt of soda water!

There are still some spots in the world where one is required to entertain oneself. It is a challenge, but in the end a lot of fun. Since Robert and Wendy had a two-hour lunch break from school they always came home for lunch. We would eat and then engage in a rousing game of croquet. We made our own rules, since our inherited croquet set had no rulebook. Robert's favorite position for shooting was lying prone on the grass and shooting as if he were playing billiards. The next most exotic playing stance was that of Lady Bromley, the British ambassador's wife. She would gracefully go down on one knee and, taking a short grip on the mallet, shoot genteelly and accurately. Our own system pleased us until the day when a guest from the University of California at Berkeley came to dine. Innocently we asked, "Would you enjoy a game of croquet with your scotch?"

"Yes, indeed, it is one of my great hobbies." Some years before, our guest had come across, quite by chance, a book in the Berkeley library by Lewis Carroll on croquet and the various ways to set up the field. "But this is no way to set up a court!" We should have taken warning then and there, as it was evident that our guest did not approve of our joyous nonchalance.

Croquet is an interesting game. One can learn a lot about people as they sneak a nudge of their ball, trip over a wicket on purpose, or accidentally play out of turn. At our New Jersey farm vineyard we now have a handsome, proper British croquet set and even had the grass court properly leveled. Sons, daughters, grandchildren, and I play a lot, always ignoring Lewis Carroll's rules.

John was also creative when it came to party giving. Though my passport says June 3, I was born on a Sunday, June 2. All those decades ago they listed the recorded day of birth, in my case, Monday, June 3. John had looked at my passport (after all we were essentially newlyweds) and my real birthday slid by unnoticed. Later, he would relate his birthday planning scenario. "Surprise party? What is that?" The manager of the Ghion Hotel, who was trying to cope with John's request to cater a party. Because his broken English was better than John's broken Amharic, they spoke English as John tried to explain the idea of "a surprise birthday party for my wife--for her day of birth."

At noon on June 3, I was lying in front of the blazing fire in our dining room. I had embarked on that most miserable of jobs, revising my address book, when I heard a terrible commotion outside our house. A cacophony of horns rang out as automobiles poured in through the iron gates, passing through the eucalyptus grove to the large parking area below our house--a real motorcade. The British ambassador led the way flying an especially large Union Jack for the occasion. They caught me in jeans and in total bewilderment. "Happy Birthday Mimi!" John immediately began pouring champagne. Then more and more champagne but no food. Finally, John confessed to me, "The food is coming from the Ghion Hotel--where the hell are their trucks?" John called the hotel. "You will get a big surprise. Truck hiding in deep woods behind your house." So he extricated the truck and the great food arrived, including five birthday cakes. By that time, however, the diplomatic corps and the university faculty were immobilized. Our children were not fit to return to school, and I, awash with champagne, friendship and my beloved husband's originality, thought it was my best birthday--ever!

One night a sort of musical chairs was the game of the evening. About thirty Ethiopians and foreigners were present, and dinner finished when John announced, "Please arrange your chairs in a circle and then sit down." All obeyed. John, a deck of cards in hand, then circled the room, assigning each guest a card suit. "You, Maria, are a heart; Jim you are a diamond; Sybil you're a spade. You must be sure and remember which suit you have been assigned. I will shuffle this deck of cards and then call out the suit of the top card. If it is your suit, you must move one chair to the left. This means that you may have to sit on someone's lap. Let's say you are a heart. Your neighbor to the left is a club. Perhaps the next card I turn up will be a club at which time you, who are a club, and your heart lap-mate will move together, one chair to the left. If the next card should be heart again, that person will move on to the next chair left. The winner is the first one to make it clear around the circle and back to his starting chair. Questions?"

There were questions galore, but gradually everyone seemed to understand and our fake game of musical chairs began amid great hilarity and confusion. Sometimes, when I recall those evenings, I regret the calm, reasoned conversations that take place at most of our parties in America. My next guests in Princeton better watch out.

10 Ī

Haile Selassie I University

Haile Selassie I University was a league of nations when John arrived to be the advisor to its first Ethiopian president. In the '60s, Americans were teaching law, business administration, and agriculture; the British gave direction to medicine; the West Germans built and administered the College of Technology; the Swedes led the Building College; and Ethiopians, in increasing numbers, were in administrative and teaching posts throughout, being trained by the foreign head of a department. No Ethiopians had attended universities until recently, as general education began by decree of the emperor in 1960. Before that time, the only citizens who studied were young men going into the church. They studied in a language called Ge'ez --a disappearing language used mainly in church liturgy. So when the university opened, it became necessary to choose a language in which there was a body of printed knowledge. The officials, or the emperor, chose English over French (the emperor's favorite language). By 1970, the faculty was equally comprised of expatriates and Ethiopians. In the beginning, John found that one of his main problems was the disparate interests and goals of the various departments and their staffs. After much discussion and backing and filling, he got the donor nations to meet regularly to analyze the university's needs and to try and do so in a cooperative spirit. "And I thought it was tough at San Francisco State!"

John's boss, the president of Haile Selassie I University, was Lij Kassa Wolde Meriam. Lij, whose name means something like "prince," was married to the emperor's granddaughter Seble, and they had six children. Lij Kassa (later Dejazmatch or Lord Kassa) was a graduate of the University of Alberta in Canada and a very nice person. He had two passions: golf and growing roses. He was not often seen at the university.

One night a handsome young Ethiopian appeared at our door in Gulele. "I am the husband of your secretary, Mr. John, and I bring you a fish which friends just delivered to us from the Red Sea." John thanked the man profusely and returned to his scotch and soda. "I am continually fascinated by these people. That man's wife is currently my secretary. She is exceptionally beautiful, but she cannot type." John had five secretaries during his tenure at the university. With fine Ethiopian features, lovely skin, long black hair dressed in the manner we associate with Nefretiti of ancient Egypt, those delightful women ranged "from gorgeous to exquisite." Each was a wife of a government official and each, in turn, was sent to John through the patronage system. "Can I get you some more coffee?" The secretary would beam at her boss as she watched him type. And John typed with two fingers. "I am the highest paid secretary of the Ford Foundation empire. Maybe when Marie leaves to have her baby, the next girl will be able to type?!" It never happened.

Then one day a crisis struck--the president of the university wanted a detailed report tollo tollo, (fast, fast). John called the American Embassy and talked to the personnel manager who ran a part-time employment service for the American community. She referred John to Miss Woizerette Wenishet who worked in an Ethiopian government office. John jumped into his Volkswagen and "beetled" off to visit Miss Wenishet. To John's surprise he was ushered past countless supplicants and lesser officials to the office of the minister himself. In Ethiopia, as in the United States, one does not wander casually into the offices of heads of government to inquire about secretarial assistance and, John told me later, "I was getting nervous about the whole business. But there, in splendid isolation sat Woizerette Wenishet, who explained that His Excellency was out of the country for several weeks and her days were free for extra work and extra pay. "Boy, am I excited. Those ministers have good secretaries--the best!"

So the next morning John hurried to the ministry with the first draft of his report. After discussing copies and margins and such, he hurried out to jump into our Volkswagen and "The damn key wouldn't work in the lock! You can picture me struggling, Mimi, and within minutes there were at least fifty Ethiopians surrounding the Volkswagen and me, blocking traffic, gesticulating, shouting advice in Amharic. One helpful gentleman disappeared for a moment and came back with a long, stiff wire. He managed to force the vent window and was just about to break the window when a middle-aged gentleman in a business suit burst through the crowd, "What the hell are you doing to my car?" John went on to recount his amazement at the violent manner of the Ethiopian, when all of a sudden the crowd began to laugh. "They were hanging on to one another, pointing to the car behind the Volkswagen I was attempting to enter--another Volkswagen identical to ours! And it was ours! Jeez, I did make a rapid departure. I don't think I'll show my face again near that ministry for a long time."

During the few months Lij Kassa and John worked together, Kassa offered my husband a tip that stood him--and me--in good stead when important world figures came to visit Haile Selassie University. "The emperor always takes university visitors to see that bust of his father, Ras Makonen. If you want to see the visitor up close, stand at the end of the corridor near the president's office and beside the statue of Ras Makonen." A number of times John alerted me when a famous person was about to descend, and I would race in from Gulele and take up my position next to Ras Makonen's statue. One day it was the tiny emperor escorting the very large queen of the Netherlands, Juliana. Another time tall Prince Phillip of England came to visit Ras Makonen, and always these guests would nod politely to John and me. We must be important to stand next the statue? Yes?

Rose Kennedy came to the university to dedicate a beautiful library in her son's memory. It was a gift from the United States. Carved in stone on its entrance hall was the famous John F. Kennedy saying, "Ask Not What Your Country Can Do For You; Ask What You Can Do For Your Country." President Kennedy's mother and the emperor were both eighty, their birthdays one day apart, and they were about the same stature. Their birthdays coincided with the dedication ceremonies. The emperor and the president's mother were everywhere together. They ignored the other dignitaries and talked quietly in a language the emperor invented (as his English was very limited). They had much to share, for they had both lived in circles of national and international power for a very long time, they had both lost their spouses, and they had both outlived beloved children. They were tiny, lone figures on the world stage.

One night John and I were dinner guests of the United States ambassador, William Hall. Bill Hall was mixing drinks in his kitchen that Sunday evening when he turned to John asking: "What am I going to do with Mrs. Rogers when the Secretary of State visits next month? As yet we haven't come up with anything that appeals to her."

John, who had been vice-president of Cornell, knew Mrs. Rogers as an alumnus and trustee of Cornell University and knew that she was very much interested in young people and education. John volunteered, "Bill, I could arrange a session with young Ethiopian professors at the university if you are both agreeable." So cables went back and forth, and the session was on; a breakfast meeting for Adele Rogers and a dozen young Ethiopian instructors. It would take place at our house to minimize chances of demonstration or disruption. For the same reason John waited until the last moment to invite the young professors, not wanting word of the meeting to get around in revolutionary circles.

Mrs. Rogers came on time. The Ethiopians did not. When they did arrive, all in their best black suits, they acted with utmost courtesy. For two hours they explained from every possible angle that the American government was making a very big mistake supporting the Imperial Ethiopian government. Mrs. Rogers tried, with intelligence and determination, to defend the United States, but the session was a standoff.

That night Ambassador Hall phoned John: "What the hell did you people talk about this morning? Mrs. Rogers was absolutely fascinated with her session with the Ethiopian instructors and professors. She couldn't talk about anything else when she caught up with the secretary."

"I am not satisfied with your answer, Aklilu," the emperor said, "Go home and think and bring me a proper answer tomorrow morning." Haile Selassie had decided to replace Lij Kassa as president of the university. Aklilu Habte was the leading candidate. He was a graduate of HSIU, and he had received a doctorate in education from Ohio State University. He was then a professor and dean at HSIU. During Aklilu's week "on trial", each morning he had a session at Jubilee Palace where, having done an acrobatic kissing of the Haile Selassie's feet, the emperor (a man of no formal education) would examine him. Aklilu had to answer in writing. When His Majesty was satisfied with his candidate's answers, he appointed him president of the university. John had a new boss.

"I wonder if we will ever have graduation this year? I long to be back in Greece and sit on the beach in Ios." John had been using all his training as a clinical psychologist to keep the international faculty from each other's throats. Even though classes and examinations were over, and everyone wanted to go home for summer, they had to wait around for two more weeks because the emperor had gone off to see President Nixon in Washington D.C. Haile Selassie had insisted on giving out all degrees personally at the university graduation ceremonies. Two weeks later his private 707 appeared on the horizon, and the next day the students of the Addis campus received their diplomas. The emperor, clad in academic robes, handing each new graduate his/her sheepskin, enquired about future plans and gave encouragement. It took hours and was followed by a luncheon in the huge dining hall.

"Why are those officers of the Imperial Bodyguard huddled together, talking so intently and looking around suspiciously? What's going on John?" After scanning the dining hall and trying to figure out the problem, my husband broke into a wide grin. "It is the emperor's dogs. You know his inseparable companions, the Chihuahuas. They seem to have disappeared." We were sitting just in front of the dais that held the emperor's dining table. Bending low to look for the dogs in a forest of human and table legs, I suddenly heard whimpering. So did the officers of the Imperial Bodyguard, who stared at the dais in consternation. The dogs were trapped under the dais. This created a terrible dilemma for the officers because lifting the dais meant lifting the emperor before hundreds of his subjects, which was totally out of the question.

Just then the daughter of a faculty member, a child of perhaps ten, jumped from her chair, ran to the dais, and went on her knees with her bottom to the skies. As the Imperial Court watched, the little girl called to the dogs through a small crack in the platform and coaxed the Chihuahuas to freedom. She became a national hero.

John flew with the emperor to all graduations. I would take him to the airport, where he and Aklilu followed the tiny royal figure down the red carpet and up the stairs. The two emperor's tiny dogs always led the way. "Every flight has two pilots, Akilu, me, and twenty men carrying ten guns." John shook his head, "Mimi, I think you should see one of those ceremonies. Why not take a commercial plane to Diri Dawa the see the graduation at the College of Agriculture?"

It was a hot, hot day and the emperor was in full regalia of commander in chief as he accepted the flowers from a little girl who was thrust forward to meet him. She was seven or eight, with lovely cafe-au-lait skin set off by her white dress. The emperor looked at her, took her by the hand and without a word to anyone, the two of them set off across the field (to see the barns and animals) with generals and courtiers and university officials bounding along behind. Haile Selassie loved being in Harrar, where he was born. On that day he was in a particularly good mood as they set off to see the cow barns, the little girl by his side. Turning to his new minister of agriculture (he frequently rotated ministers, keeping them detached by this ploy) he asked how many liters of milk the prize cow on exhibit had given. All the court began to grin, because everyone present knew that the new minister of agriculture did not know which end of the cow the milk came from!

His Majesty kept the little girl at his side throughout that graduation day at the College of Agriculture in lovely Harrar Province. When he made his long address and presented degrees to each graduate, she sat beside the lectern, her legs dangling from the platform. At the formal luncheon that followed, the emperor ordered a chair for her beside his big throne. At the end of the day when he boarded his DC-3 for the return flight to Addis Ababa, I saw the little girl standing near the runway, clutching a handful of Ethiopian dollars--a present from her emperor.

Often at those graduations I would look with admiration at the powerful yet slight figure of emperor Haile Selassie I. He had given his country a tremendous boost in donating his father's old palace to be the main building of the new university.

There was always heavy traffic around the kilos near the university--no sensible roundabout courtesy there. Besides the untrained drivers, one had the wild jitney taxi drivers who would race madly through the university gates, darting around the dividing squares up to the impressive entrance. Yet I always felt peaceful when driving through the iron gates to meet John. But all too soon this peace was shattered by student riots!

11 ፲፮

University Students Unrest

"You know Asafa Lemma, my office boy, Mimi? He came to me early this morning and said I mustn't go downtown today." John had called me at home. "You know I am supposed to take the Ford Foundation man from Nairobi out to lunch downtown. May I bring him home?" The students at Haile Selassie had been restless for some time. A member of the royal family owned the hotel where John was to have lunch, and students had smashed the large plate glass window there. Half an hour later, Asafa called John again. "It's okay to go to the hotel now, sir."

Asafa was a Tigrean from the north who somehow got to Addis and survived. His persistent ambition was to be a university student, and at age twenty-five he had finally reached the ninth grade in night school. He earned just enough to eat, and he was assigned to work for John. According to Ethiopian tradition, he was responsible to and for his master, and he waited endlessly for his master to indicate some need or whim that he could satisfy.

Hanging around the university at all hours Asafa got to know the student leaders, went to their meetings, and knew all the gossip. So, when John's phone rang at home some nights or early in the morning, he heeded attention to Asafa's warning: "Sir, this is Asafa. Sir, do not come to the university now. I will call later." As a foreign advisor John did not want to be involved in Ethiopian student politics and upheaval, and Asafa's advice was unfailingly accurate.

The assassination took place on Sunday, 28 December 1969, about 8:30 in the evening. Tilahun Gezan, president of the student body at HSIU, was standing by the road that curved around the campus and talking with his brother and a girl. When Tilahun stepped to the curb to hail a taxi for the girl, two Ethiopian men in overcoats appeared and shot him with revolvers, killing him instantly. The body was taken to the nearby Haile Selassie I Hospital, where students began to gather. At 1:30 in the morning the students stole the body and brought it in a land rover to the home of President Aklilu. The students, convinced that the government was behind Tilahun's murder, demanded that the body be protected for a proper autopsy. Aklilu immediately sensed danger ahead but decided on the spot to have the body placed under guard in the morgue that served the university medical school. It was nearly dawn then and, with Tilahun's body secured, the students dispersed. At this point Asafa called John again.

John raced to the university and into the office next to his. "We have to get out of here--now!" He was talking to Bob Geddes and his associate Barton Mix, both architects from Princeton University. They were spending their Christmas vacation at Haile Selassie I

University designing student dormitories. On his way from our house to the university John had seen thousands of students of all ages streaming towards the university. When he saw His Majesty's Imperial Bodyguard across from the main gate of the campus, "I could tell they were tense and ready to move." Driving quickly through the main gate and waving his ID card, John found thousands of students inside, huddled with friends and crying hysterically about the assassination. John ran into the office where Geddes and Mix were working, grabbed their drawings and all three got out of there in a hurry.

Later we learned that President Aklilu went to Bodyguard Headquarters in a desperate attempt to negotiate a withdrawal of their troops. While he was there, the attack began. The bodyguards killed three students and wounded scores more with bayonets and rifle butts. One teacher was shot through the leg and others clubbed and beaten. The students refused to go back to the university. Faculty, both Ethiopian and foreigners, were shocked and angry. President Aklilu pressed the students' demand for a full government investigation. It never happened. Tilahun was buried quietly at Debra Libanos, north of Addis Ababa, too far from the capital for students to attend.

When Asafa did not show up at the university John surmised that he had been arrested as a student. He found his office boy at the security guards headquarters on the Mesfin Harrar Road. Various university administrators told John there was nothing he could do. John was really angry and decided to tackle the security headquarters and eventually was allowed to see Colonel Sirak, deputy commander of the security police. Ensconced in his elegant office, in a building left by the Italians, the colonel courteously assured John "Asafa is fine. He will be back at work in a day or two." A week later John went back to Sirak: "Where the hell is Asafa?" The colonel deflected the question, saying he had recently seen John getting on His Majesty's plane. "Aha," John thought. "I will not get the runaround this time. The colonel is connecting me to the emperor. And, true to form, in a country where it is who you know with power, Sirak asked, "Would you like to see Asafa?" The young man was dreadfully pale, had a glassy stare, and mumbled, "There is nothing you can do, sir." Asafa looked sadly at John, "But thank you for coming to see me."

Back at the university a sophisticated Ethiopian came to John: "I hear the police thought they had a little fish, now they think they have a big fish. Otherwise, why would you, such an important foreigner, be interested in a simple office boy?" Asafa was released after ninety days, his feet so badly beaten he could not walk. He seemed terrified. The university did not want to give him his job back. John insisted and won.

"The revolutionary Ethiopian student movement has now reached such a high level of militancy and consciousness...it should be regarded as the prelude to the beginning of armed struggle...in our Ethiopian context, the true revolutionary is one who has shattered all sentimental and ideological ties with feudal Ethiopia...the fundamental driving force of history, and thus Ethiopian history as well, is the bitter struggle between the ruling classes and the oppressed classes..." So read part of the Marxist student publication at the university. Indeed, the USSR fanned the flames through its embassy in Addis. Its Daily News in Amharic and English informed Ethiopians over and over "that American imperialism was the main force of war and oppression." Though the student paper often attacked "the government" they never directly criticized or attacked the emperor.

It was 1970 when the weekly Addis Reporter announced, "His Imperial Majesty, in a nationwide radio and television address, granted pardon to university and other students who were sentenced to prison terms and suspended from schools for their part in the student disturbances last March [1969]." The Reporter continued, "The Emperor said he was pardoning the students 'in the firm belief that it is of paramount importance to start the New Year with a fresh spirit.' He also said, 'Foreign elements have been the cause of student disturbances....'" He admonished students "to continue and complete their education so they will have an opportunity to translate their ideas into practical realities and even introduce reforms."

It was an amazing yet ironic circumstance from an outsider's point of view. The emperor, the supreme ruler of the empire, had initiated a national education system, and understood its importance to his country. Surely he must have known it would result in the end of his sovereignty! And now uprisings in other parts of the country had commenced, uprisings by workers and peasant farmers against the emperor and against the system. These were taking place in such far-flung and disparate places as Gojjam, Bale, and Eritrea. Workers' strikes followed one after the other in Metahara, Wonji, and Akaki.

The battle lines were drawn between the Conquering Lion Of The Tribe Of Judah, Haile Selassie I, and some of his army personnel and between the "Lion" and revolutionary students. Asafa, John's office boy, was just one victim of the struggle that would bring suffering and deprivation to hundreds of thousands. Four law professors from HSIU attacked the emperor's preventive detention order as unconstitutional. Their reasoned arguments had no noticeable affect. One night John asked an Ethiopian elder, our dinner guest, why the emperor did not resign since he had no longer any effective way of governing. The old man looked at John with scornful surprise: "Emperors don't resign!"

In 1970, Ethiopia was surrounded by countries where revolution had taken place--Egypt to the north, Somaliland and Yemen to the east, Sudan to the west, and Kenya, to the south, was hardly a model for political stability. The betting among detached Ethiopians was that the royal house would fall and it would be with a resounding crash.

12 ፲፪

The Lion Of Judah

Driving back to Addis from our weekend at Lake Lugano, about two hours south of the capital, we had the misfortune of being behind Haile Selassie's car. He had spent the weekend at his Debra Zete palace. Since one could not pass the emperor's car, our progress was painfully slow, for his car stopped every time a citizen came with a complaint or request. The petitioner would simply lie down on the road, the emperor's car would stop, and an aide would take notes about the case. Progress was further hindered when the aides threw silver quarters (about the size of ours but scalloped) to people along the route.

The Lion of Judah, Haile Selassie. The name means "power of the Trinity." After all Ethiopia had been a Christian country since the fourth century. Haile Selassie's original name was Tafari Makonnen. He was the grandson of Emperor Menelik II and was educated in the French mission school. In 1928, after defeating Menelik's successor, a Moslem, Selassie installed

Menelik's daughter as empress and himself as regent. When she died in 1930, he took over as emperor.

The emperor was short, a little over five feet, and slight. He had light brown skin, piercing dark eyes, a curling beard, and an erect and regal bearing. In all the times I had been with him, I'd rarely seen him smile.

"It is an amazing experience to be with him, Mimi," John would relate. "You never hear him in conversation, though he frequently whispers something to the prime minister, you know, the one who is also the minister of the pen. What a tough job that must be! He is responsible for translating the emperor's wishes into orders, orders that could affect arrangements of the moment or the course of the empire."

The empress was long dead when we arrived in Ethiopia in 1968. Haile Selassie's favorite son had been killed in an auto accident. A daughter, a trained nurse, had died from encephalitis. The crown prince was seldom seen in public after an abortive coup a decade earlier, and he suffered a stroke during our stay in the country.

The Emperor lived in a big stone palace in Addis called Jubilee Palace. Two live cheetahs held on leash by members of the Imperial Bodyguard flanked the main stone steps, so visitors entering the palace were ever cautious. The waiting room was ornate, with settees and chairs of red velvet, and glittering chandeliers. Champagne and cigars were proffered no matter what time of day. Only one picture hung on the walls: a photograph of His Majesty with President John Kennedy on the White House steps, both smiling amiably in a moment of fun.

In 1969, the Addis Ababa Hilton opened. It had taken eight years to build, and the emperor was very proud of it. John and I, along with ambassadors, ministers and such, attended the opening festivities. Our driver, Yeardow, was embarrassed as he dropped us off in our Volkswagen amid all those Mercedes. The ballroom was magnificent. At one end, the middle of a long dais, sat Haile Selassie. His son sat to his far right (so far away they could not speak) and his daughter the same distance away to his left. Before the elegant six-course dinner began, the emperor's favorite lion was carried through the dining room. The cage was attached to two long poles that rested on the shoulders of six men--three on each side. Poor lion. He looked subdued and confused.

As I dawdled over my soup, my mind filled with images of that remarkable man's life--from his historic speech before the United Nations on 30 June 1936, to the recent founding of Ethiopia's first university. I knew that we were privileged to know him.

John and I were in the ancient city of Gondar when Neil Armstrong spoke to the world from the moon. It was 3 in the morning, but we had brought our portable radio with us so we could share that historic drama. The next morning the streets of Gondar were jammed - but it had nothing to do with the moon landing. Tens of thousands of Ethiopian peasants of all generations had flocked to Gondar by foot, mule, and bus, from many, many miles around. They had come to welcome the visiting emperor. They shrieked with joy when they saw him: "Jan Hoy! Jan Hoy!" - Haile Selassie's popular name.

Eventually, the moon landing made news in rural Ethiopia, and NASA sent out a man in space suit to lecture. In the Ethiopian countryside students at one secondary school found the idea of landing on the moon ludicrous and ran the NASA man out of town, bouncing stones off his space helmet.

Later, I would come across an excellent description of Haile Selassie, a description written some twenty-five years before, at about the time when John and I were living in Addis:

The Emperor Haile Selassie I, King of Kings and Conquering Lion of Judah, is a world statesman. His impact has been enormous; his name is known everywhere. Middle-aged Americans recall that the lead soldiers of their youth were shaped and uniformed in the likeness of his army. Everyone who watched the funeral procession of John Kennedy will remember Haile Selassie's solemn appearance as the most moving, and in some ways the most reassuring, moment of that tragic time. He presides at intervals over congresses of African states that seek to bring unity to the peoples of that continent. By his policies and position, but especially by his character, he helped powerfully to shape the conditions and new attitudes that have brought a score of black delegates to the United Nations and begun the long work of emancipating black Americans. Haile Selassie is the most powerful black man of modern times.

The overthrow of Haile Selassie's government, by a group of army sergeants, was a tragic and bitter end to his career. But that is another story, which one hopes will soon be written now that Ethiopia has returned to a legitimate government again, the "murderer," Mengistu, having fled the country.

13   ፲፫

Lalibela's Rock-Hewn Churches

"You have never seen anything in your life that remotely resembles those underground churches at Lalibela. Churches cut from living rock." The American ambassador's wife shook her head. "They put the pyramids to shame. Never mind that you can't sleep in the beds at the Seven Olives Hotel. We finally put our mattresses on the floor because they sagged so much! Aren't you and John going up there next week?" We were indeed.

John was to pay a visit to the Gondar branch of Haile Selassie University, which was located in northwestern Ethiopia. Gondar had been the capitol of Ethiopia for several centuries. On the way back to Addis Ababa we would fly into Lalibela to visit churches built in the twelfth century A.D. Until a meadow was leveled for the DC-3 planes, visitors to Lalibela arrived by donkey, a ten-day ride.

Our tiny plane flew low over the ambos (rims) flatten tops of the Semien Mountains. "Look, Mimi, there are crops growing on top of each ambo, cultivated right up to the edge of the precipice." In other places cultivation was like that of China, like ridges down the side of an ambo. We both knew that Ethiopia had been deforested over the centuries, as the royal court moved every few decades. Supporting hundreds of people, the land gradually became denuded. Addis Ababa, the twentieth century capital, was founded in the late nineteenth century.

Mimi and son Bill at one of the Seven Chruches of Lalibela

We were flying over yawning valleys that separated the highland mountains into isolated parts. After practically diving between two peaks, our plane taxied up to a circular turkel hut with a grass roof, open air Lalibela's airport building. The land rover that met us bumped over a track, climbing higher and higher up the mountainous terrain, finally reaching a village where the houses scattered along a slopping ridge. We passed the ancient olive trees, yes, seven of them, and stopped in front of a low sprawling building--the Seven Olives Hotel.

Ethiopia rises from the North African steppes and deserts like a mighty cliff-faced island. The range of high mountains in the north, which we flew over, is the heart of the ancient kingdom and where its early capital, Axum, is located. "The highest mountain is over 15,000 feet." John had been cramming! "And in the old days as there were fierce fights over succession to the throne, the man in power might isolate his opponent by putting him and his retinue on top of an ambo. Remember, we saw a village on top of one! How do you suppose people get to it?"

One of the Lalibela Priest with a distinct Lalibela Cross.

"Probably like that part of northern Greece where the monks built those incredible monasteries at Meteora. By ropes and rope hammocks. Actually, John, the land is very similar, only at Meteora the ambos are much smaller. Instead of a monastery built on a flat-topped peak, here they can build a whole village on an ambo. Look, there's another village...."

We were taken to one of the hotel's sixteen rooms and told dinner would be at six. The room was appalling. Barren, sagging beds were covered with faded bedspreads. There were no tables, nary a chair or a rug. A bald light bulb hung in the center of the room. Dinner matched, meager, all from cans. We were glad we'd brought a bottle of scotch.

"It's too late for the churches tonight. Let's take a drink, and climb up the ridge behind the hotel." John was already pouring the scotch. Although we were some 13,000 feet high, the great ranges of the Semien Mountains stretched far above our perch. Now and then an Ethiopian would pass us, climbing up the narrow path, headed home--though we could see no sign of habitation above us. Always they smiled, nodded and said, tenastiling, bowing their heads in greeting. The view was breathtaking in its unaffected grandeur. Range after range of mountains that made me think of the Tetons in Wyoming. Rugged, sharp-edged mountains. Ancient.

Christianity is essential to the very identity of the Ethiopian Kingdom and the force behind its survival for well over 1500 years. Ethiopians became Christians during the same period as the Romans, the first half of the fourth century. The Nile valley played a most important role, as the Blue Nile originates in Ethiopia's Lake Tana and flows north to join the main branch of the Nile below Khartoum.

Mimi, pointing to the external design of a church.

The connection between Egypt and Ethiopia began long before Christianity. John and I had been reading about the Coptic religion. One could not help becoming fascinated by the icons and paintings on the walls of even the smallest country church. Always those ancient Ethiopians were shown full face, with round black eyes and high foreheads. The Copts, as a people, were Egyptians from the native race descended from the Monophysite sect, believing there is in Christ but a single nature. From the third to the fifteenth century Egyptians spoke Coptic, an Afro-Asiatic language. As Islam spread through Egypt, many Copts moved south, or up the Nile River. Still today approximately 11

99

percent of the Egyptian population are Copts and practice that most ancient form of Christianity. The oldest Monophysite church, built of stone and wood, is in Cairo, dating from the sixth century and still very much in use. Later John and I would visit that church.

"It is easy to see how Ethiopia became the oasis of Christian culture." "Yes, " I answered, "and Princess Ruth says Christianity became the state religion in the fourth century, brought down from by a Roman monk who had became an advisor to the emperor. Supposedly little has been changed since the earliest centuries after Christ. I wonder how many Coptic churches are in Ethiopia? Someone told me as many as 1500."

One of the few African sects that does not bear the stigma of the white man's colonial religion, the church in Ethiopia has traditionally been the chief repository of national art, literature, and written history. Nevertheless the Coptic Ethiopian Orthodox priests, ever semiliterate, held great power. Until the eighteenth century they owned a third of the land and were deeply important to the country in many ways. Over the centuries the church gave unity to diverse tribes and language groups in a country whose rugged geography challenged any attempts for centralized government.

One day in 1971, when we were back in the States, John and I were fascinated to find a major article in the New York Times on the Ethiopian Church. The opening paragraph states:

> "Several mornings a week Alaka Baye Alemu leaves his mud-walled home in Lalibela and walks to the nearby Emmanuel Church. For three hours he reads prayers, then sets out for his day's work in the fields. Akala Baye is a forty-two-year-old priest of the Ethiopian Orthodox Church who is firmly dedicated

to "serving God and saving my soul."
Like most of his 170,000 colleagues, he
has minimal training and his is part-time
ministry.

"Would you like to go down to the market before we
visit the churches?" John asked. "It's out on that point,
beyond the olive trees."

The usually quiet village was alive with activity that
Saturday morning as we walked down the slope, past a
spring where women were patiently filling jugs from a
tiny stream of water. A short walk brought us to the
market. Covering the whole of a broad ridge, the
mountains stretching endlessly in the distance, we were
thrust into a bustling scene from, well, perhaps the
twelfth century?

Horses, goats, sheep were all for sale, as well as the
small grey donkeys of the highlands. Hundreds of
women, many dressed in rags, sat on the ground in front
of their wares that were often only a few vegetables.
Some had honey for sale, honey filled with bees. Honey
for making honey wine. Young boys, unwanted guides,
followed us. We immediately purchased wire-handled
flywhisks made from horses' tails. Flies covered every
product. The great black eyes of the small children
peered out from a mass of flies. Children so beautiful
they made my heart ache.

We were the only foreigners and people clustered
about us. Fine-featured people of every shades from light
cream to brown, filled the winding road up to the
churches, and everyone dressed in white. "John, please,
let's go back to the churches. I find it very hard to be so
much the center of attraction. If only we could
understand and talk with the people! Let's go see
Princess Ruth's house on the way to the churches. I'd
like to tell her we saw it."

How does one begin to describe one of the wonders of the world? Monuments? Living monuments? Monolithic churches carved out of a single piece of rock; free on all sides while the base rooted in living rock. There is a remarkable book called Lalibela, by George Gester published in 1970. The book has magnificent photographs. One chapter begins:

> The South Arabian moon god Almaqah made way for the 'God of Heaven,' the god of the Christians, during the reign of Ezana, king of Aksum in the first half of the fourth century. No other event in Ethiopian history can be compared with this. Upon Christianity Ethiopia based its state, society and culture. The peculiarities of its geography have successfully helped it to defend its special position as the only autochthonous [indigenous] Christian state in Africa, against all assaults, particularly those of Islam.

The Islamic conquests of the seventh century in the Near East and North Africa completely cut Axum off from the outside world, as the people of Ethiopia's northern province resisted Islam. Thus began a period of isolation for the country that lasted for centuries although Ethiopia's link to Alexandria and the church was basically preserved. The Ethiopian Orthodox Church gained its independence from the Coptic Patriarch of Alexandria in 1956.

Shortly before the middle of the twelfth century a new dynasty, the Zagwe, arose in northern Abyssinia. The center of their kingdom was a town called Roha, in the northern region of the country. One of the family, King Lalibela (1190-1225), conceived and built the churches in Roha, a town which eventually changed its name to Lalibela. Historians still have to explain how it was that the rulers of that remote kingdom, so isolated from the rest of Christendom, could have devised such a concept and carried out such an immense and difficult task. As far as I am concerned, the building of those underground churches makes the pyramids seem like child's play. One is not surprised by the idea that the Templar Knights were involved in their construction, though the church style is pure Ethiopian. (Evidence of the Templar Knights presence in Ethiopia during that time includes the appearance of the distinctive croix pattee symbol inside the churches and in and around Axum--an unusual symbol much favored by the Templar Knights.)

For some reason the language of the people was changed at this time from Ge'ez to Amharic. At the same time the Solomonic dynasty was restored, but the calendar has never been changed. John and I had a bit of a problem in Addis; when writing a letter we found it best to use two dates; the Julian calendar and our Gregorian. 1984 is our 1995. Their year begins on August 29 and each month has thirty days. The five remaining days become a thirteenth month. In our compound, it was interesting at salary time, as everyone was paid a full month's salary for that five-day month, which became a six-day month in leap years.

One of the biggest celebrations of the year was the feast of Maskal on September 19, a day commemorated as Yom Kippur in Israel. At that time of year the vibrant Maskal daisy spread its yellow blanket over most of the country. This celebration occurred just after John and I arrived in Ethiopia and were moving into our new home. The newly hired servants did tribal dances, spears in hand, all around our compound on Maskal day. There were a number of holidays in Ethiopia that, although superficially Christian, are also clearly Judaic in origin.

John and I were deeply impressed that the Ethiopian church plays such an integral part in people's lives. Everyone went to church. In the middle of the night we could hear the priests chanting in the tiny Coptic church near our home in Addis. A priest also presides at the rite of circumcision, as it is customary that all male infants be circumcised soon after birth.

Ruth Desta, granddaughter of Haile Selassie, dearly loved the churches of Lalibela. She wanted more people to visit them. If a flying field could be built, there would still have to be someplace for the visitors to stay. So that lovely young and deeply religious princess built a hotel. At first she lived with a peasant family in the village of Lalibela while village men built her a house of her own. Then the hotel was constructed, an enormous undertaking as everything had to be flown in. The hostel was simple and over the years, with many changes of manager, the rooms had become run down.

"John, would it be rude of me to suggest to Princess Ruth that the hotel needs work? I could do much of it, if she would finance the changes. I know I've never decorated anything but our houses, yet, it would be exciting to revitalize those dreary hotels rooms with some Ethiopian character, to say nothing of comfort."

John liked and admired Princess Ruth. She was principal of Haile Selassie I Girls School. She was married but had no children. The emperor had married all his children and grandchildren to leaders in the various provinces.

"I think you should go talk to her, Mimi. There is nothing to lose, and a lot of people might gain!"

Ruth was delighted by my offer. I was to do the work and she would finance my sixteen room redecorating effort. "Then," she said, smiling, "we will charter a DC-6 plane and take everything new up at the same time. It is the only way."

It took me a whole year to find, have made, and arrange for all the furnishings. The students at the handicraft school founded by Ruth's mother and run by Ruth's sister, Seble, made the wooden bed frames and basket tables. Through the one department store in Addis, I was able to buy thick pieces of airfoam rubber for mattresses, thirty-two of them! In shops along Churchill Street I found sixteen wooden headrests and son Robert drilled holes in them to make lamps. At a garage we found copper tubing that we cut in foot-long pieces, which were threaded and inserted into the holes Robert had made. Only the lamp piece with its harp and cord came from outside of the country. That is not quite true, as I had bought the thirty-two chenille bedspreads in Mombasa, Kenya because they were practical and colorful. One had to do everything oneself in Addis.

Once everything was prepared, we sent up our gardener to live for a week at Lalibela and paint all the rooms white. (Asafa had been a painter in a previous post.) It was his first plane flight and when we arrived at the hotel a week later, he was still shaken. The Ethiopian plane with the lion on its tail took Princess Ruth, John, Robert, his friend and me on the bumpy ride to the highlands. The DC-6 was a freight plane and was loaded with all the new furniture for the hotel. We five sat huddled in one corner with the furnishings, hoping they would not topple over on us if the plane hit an air pocket.

What fun we had knocking on a hotel door and announcing, "If you will let us have your room for an hour, it will be renewed." Often puzzled, guests were astounded at the change we wrought as all five of us went to work removing old furniture and then carrying thirteen new pieces--rugs, beds, lamps, pictures—into each room. Little did the guests know that one of the workers was a princess! During those few days, we all became great friends with Princess Ruth. She and Robert would sneak out for a cigarette, and we talked endlessly about the problems at the court, where she had dinner each and every night, along with all of Haile Selassie's other family members, by order of his Majesty. The feelings of foreboding were high at court. The ministers could smell the approaching trouble and everyone was jockeying for power, lining up with different adversaries of the monarch.

I stayed on in Lalibela a couple of days, after Princess Ruth, John, and the schoolboys flew back to Addis. My bedspreads from Mombasa were too wide, so I cut about a foot off each one and rehemmed them by hand. When I got back to Addis, I sewed those long strips together. They made perfect picnic throws.

Every evening of those lonesome days in Lalibela I would walk down the slope, marvel at the churches and the village people, descendants of ancient Egypt whose way of life went virtually unchanged over the centuries. Often I would encounter a priest, austere in his robes and white turban and always carrying his umbrella, even in the late afternoon. Some of the umbrellas were black, but often each panel was a different color velvet and fringed around the edge. Even in very old paintings of Ethiopian life, people carry umbrellas, though those appear to me to be woven of some reed.

Often I have wondered about my churches, as members of the royal family were imprisoned in 1974 by Mengistu and the endless number of Ethiopians put to death during the years of communist rule. Princess Seble, during her visit to my farm told me the churches are doing well. The hotel still exists and, I knew that one miraculous day, I would visit them again.

14. ፲፬

Two Historic Towns—Harrar And Gondar

Blood streamed down John's forehead. He stumbled out of the marketplace in Harrar and took a taxi to the College of Agriculture in the nearby town of Alemmaya. The dean, Makonnen Kebrit, took one look: "What happened?" John shook his head, "You won't believe me but I was attacked by a chicken!" "A chicken?" Makonnen asked in disbelief. He was a graduate of Cornell's College of Agriculture, and he knew what chickens did and did not do. They did not attack people.

It is conjectured that Harrar had been a Christian city taken over by a colony that migrated from Southern Arabia and introduced Islam sometime between the seventh and ninth centuries. An ancient, walled city with narrow winding streets, Harrar is mostly populated by the Haraghi, a unique people with their own language, customs, and dress. It is one of Ethiopia's thirteen provinces located in the southeast, and the city was just beginning to modernize, its branch of the national university leading the way.

After breakfast at our hotel in Harrar, John and I had decided to take a walk through the old city. One of John's jobs at Haile Selassie University was to make a development plan for the future. We had driven down to Harrar province to spend a week and John would meet with the officials of the Agricultural College. There were many attractions in the old city of Alemmaya--great stonework, a colorful outdoor market, woven baskets and mats, slender women in bright dress, said to be the most beautiful in all of Ethiopia.

As we walked on a narrow path between high stonewalls, a white chicken, screeching and cackling, suddenly flew onto John's head. Her talons, or whatever chickens have, lacerated John's forehead and blood streamed down his face. At the college Dean Makonnen was very concerned and saw that John was cleaned up, but he could not stop shaking his head and laughing, "A chicken! An attacking chicken!"

The fingers of the Harrar Mountains stretch toward the Gulf of Aden, dividing the Great Rift Valley from the plains of the Ogaden desert region. On the top of those mountains is the coffee-growing region of Ethiopia, and a great deal of chat is grown there too. Everyone at the college was eager to increase our very limited knowledge of that part of Ethiopia.

On our second night in Harrar, Makonnen suggested that we take a mysterious trip out to the desert. It was moonless dark, and we drove a few miles, then sat with our headlights on. After fifteen minutes or so two yellow, luminous dots appeared in the night. Then another pair of shining dots, another and another. Soon the Hyena Man of Harrar, sitting on the ground and in the headlights of our car, was surrounded by circling, snarling hyenas. He tossed them some chunks of meat.

Then he held up some pieces of meat and the most aggressive hyenas approached warily and snatched them from his hands. Finally, the Hyena Man held meat between his teeth and waited until one of the big, ugly animals came and took it – mouth to mouth.

On our last day in Harrar, John and I drove east, through barren country sparsely inhabited by Muslims and their camels. We went to see the Valley of the Rocks--sometimes called the Valley of Marvels. These are fantastic formations of huge rocks balanced on top of one another, many looking like enormous phallic symbols replete with gigantic stone testicles. "What a variety of topography in Ethiopia. For a relatively small country it boasts just about everything." John shook his head.

The country in Harrar province has a very different history from that of the highlands. It is on the trail of a very ancient trading route between India, the Middle East, and Ethiopia. All the country's salt comes in through Harrar, great chunks loaded onto donkeys or camels that plod in caravans from the area of the province that is below sea level. Ethiopia's biggest export is the leaf of the plant I discussed earlier--kat or chat. The hot, hot climate of southern Ethiopia contrasts with the climate of Addis, which is at an altitude of 8,000 feet altitude and has the "little rains" of spring and the "big rains" of summer. The barrenness of the southern lands made us feel that we had come to a different world. The Muslims had tried hard, at least in the Harrar area, to convert people to their religion.

Guidebooks do not do justice to the main attraction of the Valley of the Rocks but they do describe the city of Jigjigga that lies about thirty-five miles beyond the valley and against the foothills of the Harrar Mountains. This is where Ethiopia's desert fades into the Somali desert. Beyond Jigjigga is a vast plain that eventually merges into the Ogaden. Jigjigga offers Somali handicrafts for anyone who reaches that remote place. Jigjigga also offered smuggled electronics and whisky and other goods for the large Ethiopian Army contingent stationed there. It was not an area John and I would return to -- given a choice. The northern part of the country is far more inviting.

One of the famous Gondar Castles

Like a thousand Grand Canyons! That's what it looks like flying over northern Ethiopia--"The Roof of Africa." Flying over the Semien Mountains affords the passenger a magnificent sight with each successive peak a little higher, a darker shade of purple. The Ethiopian Airlines DC-3 landed on a grass strip and taxied up to

the circular turkel hut that served as terminal for the town of Gondar. Early in the sixteenth century, following devastating wars with the Muslims, the Galla people of southern Ethiopia began massive a migration north, pushing the highland Ethiopians before them. In order to avoid the Galla onslaught, King Susenyos moved his capital to the northern shore of Lake Tana in the northwestern part of the country. When the King's son, Fasilidas, ascended the throne, he moved the capital further north and expelled the last of the Portuguese missionaries, ridding the Gallas of Catholic influence. Fasilidas built himself a magnificent castle, still the most magnificent of Gondar's several castles, and decreed that no foreigner might live in the new city. Another city, Addis Alem, rose up to the south of Gondar to house all the Persians, Indians, and

Armenians who had found their way to Ethiopia. So kings of Ethiopia came and went, some died a natural death, others were poisoned or assassinated, often in the name of religion. But Gondar remained the capital of Ethiopia until the mid-eighteen hundreds.

Mimi in Harar

Several times John and I journeyed north to Gondar with its historic castles, reminding one of that gentle city's medieval glory. Capital of Begemeder Province, the Gondar of today is a clean, quiet town nestled among the foothills of a high plateau. The Public Health College of the national university was located in Gondar, hence our visits. While there we also visited one of the most famous churches in the country--the Debre Berhan Selassie Church with murals some 300 years old, said to be the best of Ethiopian religious art.

"Let's visit Lake Tana, John. It looked so inviting from the plane." So we drove, on mostly empty roads, to the shores of Lake Tana, the source of the Blue Nile. The Blue Nile travels southward over the spectacular Tissisat Falls before heading westward to Khartoum. As we picnicked by the falls, daughter Wendy took a stroll only to return screaming, "I saw a snake. A huge snake. Why am I always the one to see snakes? I hate them so!!!" It was true that wherever we ventured in Ethiopia, Wendy would see a snake, though John and I never saw a single reptile.

Driving from Gondar one day "just to see the countryside," we encountered a beautiful, dark-skinned woman standing by the roadside, obviously wanting us to stop to buy her wares. She had a small Star of David molded from clay and dung. We bought a number of primitive figures—a pregnant woman, a couple in the martial bed, a crouching lion, and a family around a table. This handsome woman was a Falashas. The Falashas are a people who lived, during our years in Ethiopia, just north of Lake Tana. They are Ethiopians of "Agaw" stock, and they practice a peculiar kind of Judaism. Falashas is a Semitic word that appears to connote "emigrant". They established themselves in the area of the Semien Mountains in the fourteenth century. Scholars claim that their beliefs embody a curious mix of pagan-Judaic-Christian beliefs and ceremonies. We bought a number of the clay figures, which averaged six to eight inches in length and they continue to remind us of the complexity of Ethiopia's ethnic and religious diversity.

I suppose the foremost creation in Ethiopian literature is the story of King Solomon and the Queen of Sheba. This legend has been woven into Ethiopian life in the most intimate manner throughout the centuries and is depicted in much of their artwork. The story goes like this. The Queen of Sheba visited King Solomon, bore him a son, who became Ethiopia's Menelik I, and goes on to tell how the son visited his father and abducted the Ark of the Covenant, which was taken to Axum, the new Zion. This legend was committed to writing in the fourteenth century; its purpose, no doubt, was to lend support to the claims and aspirations of the recently established Solomonic dynasty.

I read recently a statement about Ethiopia that, in a way, says it all:

Ethiopia, during the reign of Haile Selassie, advanced more in fifty years than it had during the 3,000 years between Menelik I and Menelik II."

John and I arrived during that fifty years.

15

Our Children, Hijacked

"Mother said it was less than an hour's flight, Mike. I think we are way over that." Our daughter Helen and our son Bill were traveling with Mike, a young professor on the plane to Dire Dawa. Mike looked at Helen in amazement. "Didn't you know, Helen? We've been hijacked!"

John and I had driven our son and daughter to the airport in Addis Ababa early that July morning in 1969. They were going down to visit friends of ours who taught at the Haile Selassie University branch in Dire Dawa in eastern Ethiopia. "It will be interesting for you to see another part of Ethiopia while you're here," John said. " After all, you may never be in this part of the world again."

To get to Ethiopia son Bill had flown from west to east, across Africa, from Upper Volta to Kenya, where we met him. He was doing a two-year stint in the Peace Corps and had been assigned to teach in West Africa. The Peace Corps asked that their teachers not leave the continent on their month's holiday and Bill was lucky to have parents living in Africa. Helen, a teacher, had flown from the United States to spend her holiday with us.

It was midafternoon of that same July day when an American in the employment of Ethiopian Airlines (run at that time by TWA) called our home in Addis. "I have called to let you know the Ethiopian flight from Addis to Dire Dawa was hijacked. All we know so far is the plane was taken to Aden in Yemen."

John and I were frantic, even though Helen and Bill were in their midtwenties, being hijacked was a scary event! Eritrea is the northern part of Ethiopia, and many of the people are Muslim. For some time the Eritrean Liberation Front had been causing problems, threatening to withdraw from the rest of the empire. Indeed, years later they did just this, but in the late 60s and early 70s Ethiopian Airlines carried two policemen on each flight to prevent hijacking.

Bill Hall, the American Ambassador to Ethiopia told us that the United States had no representative in Aden. Ethiopian Airlines had no communication with their crew. John went to the university to look for help, and an Ethiopian friend picked up the phone and called a cousin who lived in Aden. By coincidence the cousin had talked with some of the hijacked passengers. That is how we found out that our children were definitely OK.

That night a telegram arrived: "WITH THE BRITISH NOW EVERYTHING OK." It was signed "Bill." Thank God, we said, the British in Aden have taken the passengers under their wing. It took three days for the Ethiopians to negotiate the passengers out of Muslim Yemen. John and I were besieged by embassies and press who wanted to talk to Bill and Helen upon their in Addis. So my offspring held a sort of press conference at our home, describing how the plane had been hijacked by two young men from the Eritrean

Liberation Front who carried hand grenades and guns. When the unscheduled plane landed in Aden, a plain-clothed Ethiopian security man on board killed one of the hijackers. Then the Adenese soldiers started firing around the plane. The passengers quietly disembarked and ran for cover.

"What about the British?" a member of the press asked at the end of the interview. "Did their consul really help you?"

"Oh," said Bill, "The British with us were other hijacked passengers who were staying at the hotel where some of us had been taken. I was drinking beer with them when one of them suggested I could send a telegram to my family."

But it was after the press left our living room that Bill and Helen began to tell the details of their adventure.

"I was sitting in the rear of the plane," Helen said going to describe the configuration of the DC-6. "I was across the aisle from your professor friend, Mike, and his seven-year-old daughter. Bill was sitting a few rows behind us, reading Theodore White's The Making of a President. It seemed to me that we had flown well over an hour, and below us I could see water, and I was pretty sure there were two lakes on the way to Diri Dawa. That's when I turned to Mike, saying, 'Mom told us it was a short flight...'"

Mike continued to look at Helen in amazement. He pointed, " See that young man sitting on the arm of the front seat. He's holding a hand grenade. The stewardess whispered to me a few minutes ago. The other hijacker is up with the pilot." Helen got up and went back to see Bill and tell him of their plight. "Oh? We are? Hijacked?" And Bill, all 6'4" of him, got up to look out the window. "Sit down!" the stewardess ordered. "I just wanted to get a map to see where Aden is." Bill sat back down, just as

117

the hijacker was passing a basket of hard candies around to the passengers.

Helen had on a miniskirt dress, striped in three colors and was carrying a white silk shawl. Bill advised her, "Helen, cross you legs and put that shawl over them. That hijacker in front seems to be peering up your dress. Maybe you should go up and distract him." Exasperated Helen asked, "Where the hell is Aden?"

"You know, Helen, before I left Upper Volta I went to see a "diviner," you know, a sort of soothsayer, and she told me a I would meet a woman and have a "fling" and then go on a trip where there would be rugged mountains."

"Well", Helen said, "Ethiopia has rugged mountains. We are flying over them. Did you meet the woman and have a fling?"

"Yes, but that is a story for another day."

Soon they landed, desert all around, brown earth, and brilliant blue sky.

Bill continued: "Later we found out the hijackers wanted to fly to Mogadishu in Somalia, disembark the passengers and blow up the plane. I guess the pilot convinced them he would have to land in Aden for fuel. The Yemenis apparently didn't know what to make of the unexpected plane, but they soon surrounded it with soldiers carrying rifles." He got up and made it to the restroom, where he could hide and watch. The stewardess came and said the emergency windows were open and they should climb out. "No way," I called out to Helen. "We could be shot. I hear shots all the time. Maybe they are shooting passengers as they disembark?"

Helen had noticed a very tall man in a dark suit and had wondered if he was one of the two security men we had told her accompanied every Ethiopian Airline flight. Just then he rose and fired down the aisle and hit the first hijacker in the arm. He fell near Helen's feet and at that point Bill yelled, "Hit the floor!" "I tried to fling myself down," Helen giggled, "but my seat belt was on." Finally, undoing her seatbelt, she lay on the floor between seats, covering her face with her shoulder bag. "Bill was squished in between seats, lying on the floor too, and then the hijacker who had been shot in the arm got up and tried to get off the plane. When he went down the stairs one of the security agents shot him again and again." The other hijacker jumped out the pilot's door and was captured.

"Mike yelled at us, 'Let's go!' The stewardess, Mike, his daughter, Helen, and Bill raced down the steps. Mike yelled, 'If you can hear the shot, it hasn't hit you...run!' It must have been 120 degrees. Hot as hell and the heat reflected off the tarmac in waves and people looked fuzzy. The whole scene was surreal." Bill shook his head as he recalled the scene. "Chaos!"

"By that time jeeps with soldiers had surrounded the plane and a jeep arrived to take passengers to the terminal, where we were put on buses and taken into town to a handsome, slightly run-down hotel left over from the colonial period, a hotel out of a Joseph Conrad novel. Outside stood a Chinese guard. We had forgotten that communist China was a big influence on Aden."

"The hotel was virtually empty, and we were each given a private room and left to wander anywhere we liked. One day the hotel treated us to a minibus tour of North Yemen. This was in the evening, because every morning we were all taken back out to the airport, where they stamped our passports with exit visas. Then we would adjourn to the airport bar and hang around the whole day. We learned a lot about each other. I guess the authorities hoped to get the plane released, and we'd be on our way. One airline person kept coming to reassure us. We had elegant meals, waiters in tuxedos and lived on "shandys" -- lemonade and beer together. It

119

was better than plain beer. It was so hot that the beer had no head. Frequently an airline person would reassure us: 'Don't worry, we are paying for everything and trying hard to get you home'".

Every night there Helen rinsed out her dress and hung it up to dry. "It was like being suspended in time, though I was never frightened. But we all fretted because we were told the pilots and stewardesses were in jail." The English consul, complete with mutton-chop sideburns and droopy mustache, had wanted to detain one of the English passengers from the flight--keep him in Aden long enough to question him, since the hijacker, grenade in hand, had sat on the arm of the young Englishman's seat during the drama. Bill protested. "I will not leave unless we all go--all together." Ethiopian airlines could not fly the original plane back to Addis. It had too many bullet holes, but they brought another plane. The negotiators had "negotiated" the pilots and stewardesses out of jail. Armed with box lunches and soda pop, the passengers climbed aboard, greatly relieved. An hour-and-a-half later the scene at the Addis airport was sheer emotional drama as relatives and press--much of it international-- mingled to greet the returning heroes. Bear-hugging our offspring we headed for the quiet of our stone-towered home, where we drank gin and tonics and heard Bill and Helen's odyssey. I do not recall that we ever asked ourselves "What the hell are we doing in Ethiopia?" Our adventures must be akin to our ancestors conquering of the western United States.

16   TI

Camping In The Great Rift Valley

There they were again--staring at us. John and I were trying out the idea of a picnic once a week, and chose Entoto, the impressive mountain rising behind Addis Ababa, for our first outing. "It will be ideal," John had said. "It's really deserted up there, and we can drink some wine, talk, and watch the city below." A long, wide street climbs the slopes of Entoto, going around a number of kilos (roundabouts). Just past sidist kilo (sixth roundabout) one passes the American Embassy on the right and Haile Selassie University on the left. Stopping where the paved street ran out, John and I walked into the woods, where we found any number of neat-looking picnic spots. We settled in, but within minutes Ethiopians emerged from the eucalyptus forest in their white shamas, singly, in small groups, adults and children. They never approached us directly, just stood and stared. It happened like this on all of our travels throughout Ethiopia, even in the most remote places. Gradually we learned to live with being observed whether putting up a tent, swimming, or eating.

It was hard, in many ways, living in Addis Ababa. Though the city is beautifully situated, the massive poverty of its people often made foreigners uncomfortable, particularly since there was little one could do about it.

Following the example of the Leitheads, who we often accompanied, we began taking camping trips most weekends. It seemed an ideal way to explore the country, and we had been able to buy some equipment from departing army personnel. With two tents and a couple of boxes of pots and pans, we set off. At first we only went as far as Lake Lungano, about two hours south of Addis, but it had a small hotel and too many campers and so, with Gaby's help, we began to explore the string of lakes to the south of Addis.

The Great Rift Valley begins in the Arabian Peninsula, crosses under the Red Sea, cuts across Ethiopia and ends in Uganda. In some places in northern Ethiopia the valley is below sea level. But when it reaches central Ethiopia this great scar on the earth's face is high land and dotted with lakes. Many of the lakes have a major problem. If you swim in them you might get a disease called balharsia, a blood disease caused by a parasite that makes its home in snail shells and can burrow under a person's skin. The disease is well known to the people of Egypt and Ethiopia. All the Rift Valley lakes had been tested, and we were told in which of them we could safely swim. So began our trial and error excursions as we set out to find our favorite "safe" lake. Its name was Shalla.

It took us several hours, driving south, to reach the unmarked track that led us through meadows, in and around stands of thorn acacias and the mud castles of termites and finally to the shore of Lake Shalla. The moment our car stopped we were surrounded by young Galla men with their one-shoulder-covered garment, each proudly holding a spear that was as tall as the man. By some mysterious means, John and Charles Leithead would choose a guard from among these young warriors even before we began to erect our tent.

One or more of us would take the car and penetrate the thick woods to the east in search of the ever-elusive spring where we would fill our ugly, plastic water jugs. Overhead, chattering and leaping from tree to tree, would be the small colobos monkeys, their long silky black and white fur strikingly contrasted against the sky. Jugs filled at the cool, quiet spring pool, we would head directly back to the lake, past a few poor farms with their banana trees and along the lakeshore. The back of our station wagon served as storage for all food, as it was easy to shut up at night.

The balarsia-free water of Shalla was the most peculiar color. High in iron content, it looked rather like strong tea. The shade was not particularly conducive to swimming, but swim we did. I always had a feeling that some prehistoric monster was submerged in the deep of the lake and was observing our antics.

Twilight is early on the equator, and dark comes suddenly. Even so, that hour before night was magical. The look of the ancient stones always made us aware how close we were to Lake Rudolf and the area where, in the 1960s, the Leaky family discovered bones belonging to earliest human on earth. Then there was the knowledge that we were very far from what is called the "civilized world," that we were in a simpler world, where little had changed for centuries untold, where, in the evening, the sky would become vivid pink as the greater flamingoes flew overhead, hunting for their evening's resting place. A dozen glorious white pelicans would swim by in wedge formation, diving in unison in search of the last fish of the evening.

When son Bill and daughter Helen visited, the summer of the hijacking, we borrowed another tent and took them to Lake Shalla. Wendy and Helen shared quarters, and in the morning they discovered that their tent had been split at ground level, and that someone had reached in, taken their purses, taken out the money, and returned the bags. "It's really scary to think someone was right there by our heads! Where was our guard?" John confessed: "When it started to rain, I suggested he spend the night in the Volkswagen." Another time, Wendy emerged from her tent screaming, "It bit me! An ant bit my nipple, and there is a whole army of ants marching around the inside of our tent!" Put alongside so much beauty, the chance to live simply and pretend we were pioneers, a few ants and robbers were nothing.

On the first morning of each and every camping trip we shared with the Leitheads, we awakened to see dozens of Ethiopians sitting in the dirt under the thorn-acacia trees, waiting for the doctor to wake up and come out of his tent. Some were shivering; others were motionless. Many had walked or been carried miles after the word spread during the night that our doctor friend had arrived for a weekend's camping.

Charles Leithead had decided years before that the best way to deal with the situation was to do a rapid triage, passing by the dying and the fit, administering quinine and other medicines to those who might be saved. Then the guard we had hired would turn everyone away so Charles could get some rest from his day-and-night medical practice in Addis.

Gastroenteritis, malaria, bilharzias and other parasites, pneumonia, measles. polio, and other diseases were widespread in the country--even before the terrible famines of the 70s and 80s. Infant mortality was staggering. All foreigners boiled and filtered their drinking water, and we had all had the shots then available against things like measles and polio.

On the fourth of July, we Americans were celebrating at Lake Shalla with two packages of sparkles we had conned off an American army friend. They were for our son, John Paul Summerskill, age four. "King of the Sparklers", that's what we called him, and the Ethiopians stood near the edge of the trees looking in awe as the brilliant sparks cut patterns in the African night.

Gradually, we became braver and ventured to some of the lakes south of Lungano and Shalla. Lake Abaya is a very large lake, and our destination as we headed to southeastern Ethiopia near the Kenya border. This area is very different from northern Ethiopia's high altitudes. As we neared the Kenyan border the air was hot and humid, thick tropical vegetation pressed in from all sides. Near the town of Arba Mench we headed for Lake Abaya, which lies between the provinces of Gomu Gofa and Sidamo. There was a boat to take us to the far side of the lake. We, along with the new Amharic governor who had just been assigned to a remote district across the lake, waited in the shade of a large tree. The boat arrived, and we helped the governor and his wife load their possessions--a wooden bed frame, a couple of chairs, and a few boxes. When we climbed aboard the rusted, steel landing craft, the heat was intense. That's when my fair-skinned husband uncorked the sun blocking lotion and the baldheaded governor held out his hand for a squirt.

The village population had gathered on the landing dock on the far side of the lake. The women stared at me, taking in every detail of my denim skirt and blouse, and I stared back at their skirts. We smiled at each other, a woman's smile. Then I remembered a bunch of balloons in my purse. John and I blew them up, tied knots, and gave them out. Adults rushed past their children to get a balloon. It was all a mistake, though, when we discovered the governor and his wife sitting sourly aside, the limelight stolen by the balloons, and I had none left! Diving into my purse, I found a corkscrew with a Greek god's head stamped on its handle. With as much ceremony as we could muster, this was presented to the governor. Fortunately for us, none of the balloons burst while we were present.

On a side trip from Lake Abaya we drove along a dirt trail by a lovely tropical stream. When we came to a clearing, a sandy riverbank, we thought of returning to pitch our tents there the following night. On the way back we stopped at a little pump house to ask for a refill of our canisters. John asked the guard about camping by the river. He shook his head and clapped his hands together in an unmistakable imitation of crocodile jaws. Everyone in our party knew about the American Peace Corps volunteer who had been eaten by an Ethiopian crocodile.

In that particular safari we tried an experiment: Did the Ethiopians we met in faraway Gomu Gofa know the emperor? We tried, in every language our party could muster, including Swahili and Amharic, to find some recognition of the emperor of their country. No one reacted to the name Haile Selassie.

Further on south in the border province of Bale, a mountainous, rugged area of southeast Ethiopia, we nearly got ourselves in serious trouble. Bale had only recently been opened to travel when the government in Addis negotiated an amnesty with local shiftas (bandits) who turned in their rifles. Blithely John and I set out, with another American couple, as if on a drive to the corner store. We had no provisions, no warm clothes, and there were certainly no gas stations. John was driving a borrowed Mercedes station wagon, carefully negotiating curves with one eye on the ditch and the other alert for trucks hauling huge logs down the mountainside. "Whoops, something's wrong!" he cried as he braked to a halt. We all got out to stare gloomily at the punctured tire. That's when I noticed a drip, an ominously constant drip from the rear of the car where the gas tank was located. The tank, like the tire, was punctured. There we were in wild unknown country, no probable help for days. Sometimes I thank God for my western childhood when flat tires and such were common. I remembered that chewing gum could fix the gas tank leak, but who had gum? Our friends produced two packets of Wrigley's Spearmint and we all chewed like mad. "You must chew until all the sugar is gone." Soon we plugged the leak, the men changed the tire, and we went merrily on our way again.

Our time in Ethiopia was drawing to a close. Little did we suspect what impact those years would have on our lives--and those of some of our children. Popular wisdom says that time spent in Africa impacts one's life forever. It obviously impacted mine or I would not be writing this manuscript. One of my sons, Bill, has been an African Art Dealer and collector for more than twenty-five years. "Ethiopian Art" is the show currently displayed in his New York gallery. Robert, my youngest son, took a job in Zaire when he finished university. After spending a month in South Africa this past winter, I met Bill in Addis Ababa, and so, twenty-five years later, returned to the ancient Christian land that had been so important in John's and my life.

17   ፲፯

Ethiopia Revisited

Until a few minutes ago I sat in the deep armchair that now lives in my bedroom, a wedding present from fifty years ago. I have been reading my Ethiopian manuscript cover to cover. My canopied four-poster bed comforts by its mere presence, a tidy little fire blazes in the Franklin stove in the corner of my bedroom. My eyes wander to John's written proposal of marriage, which I keep close by my desk. I dream and try to connect my recent time in Ethiopia with the life John and I led there so many years ago.

Twenty-five years have passed since John and I left Ethiopia and settled on a thirty-acre farm near Princeton, New Jersey. John became head of the college boards at the Educational Testing Service, near Princeton, and we cared for our sixteen head of cattle. Then, in 1985 we moved for six years to Greece, where John was the president of Athens College. During those years I founded and ran a student program in Kenya, always longing to visit Ethiopia. It was impossible as the dictator, Mengistu, was running the country. But the

Princeton farm was our root and, each year during spring vacation at Athens College, we returned to New Jersey and planted 2,000 Seyval Grape vines. In 1985, with 10,000 vines in place, John gave up education and became a full-time farmer, and we built a winery. I use my maiden name again, LaFollette, as labeling on wine bottles!

With educating children and nurturing grapes, we

Mimi and her son, revisiting.

never returned to Ethiopia, though it was often in our thoughts as it passed through times of horror. However, last year, Bill's collection of Ethiopian art was brought together at his Soho gallery for an exhibition, and those handsome artifacts were the inspiration for me to take Bill and revisit my past. So twenty-five years later I returned to all the places I loved in the ancient Kingdom of Ethiopia, and I share my adventures and discovery of modern Ethiopia with my readers.

Over the decades I have met my five children in remote airports, in train stations, and on ferryboats. Somehow these prearranged meetings have always worked. Still, it seemed remarkable to me, having just spent two weeks more-or-less unreachable on safari in Kenya, that when I arrived at the Ghion Hotel in Addis Ababa in late November, 1995 the desk clerk said casually, "Oh, yes, Mrs. Summerskill, your son arrived a couple of hours ago. He is in your room." How appropriate for Bill and me to be staying at the old Ghion! After all it was where John, the younger children, and I had lived several weeks in 1968 while house hunting in Addis Ababa.

"Let's take a walk, Bill. Maybe the emperor's old stables are still next door?" Strolling up the long drive that winds through the grounds of the Ghion, we encountered two young Ethiopians, laundry workers from the hotel. "We don't know about the stables, but just up this hill is the Bhata Church, where all the recent emperors are buried, including Haile Selassie. "The church just opened three days ago as Mengistu closed all of our churches". As Bill and I approached the round turkel-like church, a group of about sixty white-clad Ethiopian women, shamas gracefully draped around their heads and shoulders, approached the church, knelt and kissed the ground and proceeded inside. They looked like a flock of angels.

"Oh, Bill, it's moving to see these deeply religious people able to live freely again. It has been such a difficult time for historic Ethiopia, including the times of famine. Did you know that some people even blame Mengistu for the famine as he tried to force on farmers what to plant when and where."

"Where is the so-called murderer now? " Bill asked.

"He escaped to a West African country, and the New York Times recently reported that Mengistu survived an assassination attempt there."

Wandering back to our hotel, Bill and I found our way to the Ghion's Ethiopian restaurant (having first been seated in the western dining area), and so ate our injera and wot on a round basket table. "Bill, I can hardly contain myself, I am so eager to see our old house. After all it was considered the handsomest house in Addis."

"Mom, I remember it well, after all I spent a month there with you and John. Let's get a cab tomorrow morning and see if we can find it. If we don't you're never going to enjoy our days on the historic trail."

The driver knew the Ambo Road and I remembered the Pasteur Institute on that road near our house. Only minutes later we found that fabulous compound that was "home" for several years. The keeper of the great iron gates threw them back for us (I wonder who he thinks we are?), and we passed through the eucalyptus grove and parked in the large area below the brick steps leading up to the house. Everything was exactly the same. The zoolike sturdy lion cages were still empty, as was the massive aviary structure. In my head I peopled the lawn to the left with Wendy and Robert, John and Mimi gathering for a daily croquet game.

A Swiss legation of some kind occupies "my" house now. They administer orphanages and hospitals all over Ethiopia. Inside all looked the same, except that the kitchen was a proper, Western kitchen now with built-in cupboards and all. "This is our guest room," the handsome Swiss lady said, patiently humoring my curiosity. It was John's and my old bedroom suite.

The travel office at the Ghion was not reassuring about our flight to Gondar, which was to be the first stop on our pilgrimage. "Sometimes the plane leaves at ten in the morning, but if they have all the seats filled, they take off early. I think you should get to the airfield very early--and hope." The colorful airplane, painted red, green, and yellow (Ethiopia's national colors), looked exactly like the ones twenty-five years ago--and are probably the same planes! We got on the flight, which did leave early, and shortly Bill and I found ourselves in Gondar. As advisor to the president of the national university of Ethiopia, John had to visit all the campuses several times a year. The Gondar campus of Haile Selassie University now trains doctors and nurses. The Ghion hotel chain has built a new hotel in Gondar, a big improvement from the tiny rundown hotel where John and I had stayed. The Goha is on a ridge high above the world. The view out across the foothills (some foothills!) of the Semien Mountains was a pastel painting in blues, greens, and purples. Driving through town I spotted two enormous stone-carved lions. "Guarding a garage? I wondered where they began their lives."

I had forgotten the one-horse-two-wheel carts. Five or six Ethiopians squished into a cart built for two. The coat hooks at the Goha Hotel were actually cow horns. Before dinner Bill and I walked down the dirt road that snaked up the steep hill, encountering school children with book bags, shyly looking at the "ferenges". A mother came toward us, holding a five-year-old boy's hand. Suddenly she paused, took his head between her hands and turning it from side to side kissed him again and again. "Of course, one always kisses at least three times. I had forgotten. Why are all Ethiopian children so huggable? Is it those great round eyes? And how do the women keep their white dresses and shamas so white?"

Bill and I spent two days visiting the massive stone castles at Gondar. The Gondar of today is a clean, quiet town nestled among the foothills of the plateau. Here is some of the most dramatic scenery of the Ethiopia highlands, its emerald hills falling away to limitless vistas. One could see why King Fasilidas chose Gondar, on the shores of Lake Tana, as the location of his seventeenth century palace. Subsequent monarchs built castles, including Yasu II, who had one room of his palace entirely paneled in ivory. Yasu II was the last king before the dissolution of Gondar. So we wandered, history book in hand, among the ten picturesque castles and ruins inside of a high stone wall. "I particularly want to see Fasilidas Baths, Bill." That small stone castle has arched doorways and windows and wooden balconies hanging over the baths. "It looks more like a small lake to me. Can you picture King Fasilida cavorting there with his girl friends? Anyone this fond of luxury must have had many a mistress."

It was a short flight from Gondar to Lalibela, swooping up and over the edge of Lake Tana. We flew low over the green and brown checkerboard fields. "Isn't it fascinating how many shapes a field can take? You would never realize it except from the air." Over flat-topped ambos (ridges) often cultivated, over streams, stands of trees, and dozens of villages. Mostly the people still live in round turkel houses with grass roofs. "Sometimes I can't tell a haystack from a home." But some of the village people have gone "modern" and built a square house, using sheets of corrugated tin as roofing.

The airport building at Lalibela was also made of corrugated tin-- not just the roof, but the sides as well. Close by, however, was the old turkel airport building that I remembered so well. Its grass roof was about to collapse, but the wooden seats around the edge, were as sturdy as ever.

A bus waited on the small grass airfield to take Lalibela visitors over the narrow winding fifteen-mile ride up and up and up to the mountainous area of the famous churches. "One can walk—a good three-and-a-half hour climb," said the driver shaking his head. "But some people still do it, even today." When John and I first visited Lalibela with Princess Ruth she often referred to the days before Ethiopian Airline began its flights "We had to go by donkey, and it was a six-day trip from Debre Tabor to Lalibela."

"Bill, it looks exactly the same! And the only really positive thing one can say about The Seven Olives Hotel is-- what a location!'" Imagine my amazement when I realized that the beds in our room were my beds--the ones I had ordered twenty-five years ago. And they squeaked every time one turned over. The large turkel-shaped dining room was unchanged, except that the food was much improved. Bill and I sat outside on the wide terrace having a drink before dinner. I had sat for days on end there hand-hemming the thirty-six chenille bedspreads from Kenya. "They were all different colors, Bill, and I thought they would be easy to care for." Bill was not that interested in nonexistent bedspreads. "What a location!" He shook his head, "I feel as if we are on top of the world."

Our first night in Lalibela, Bill and I made a friend who then joined us at mealtime. He was an Ethiopian, but from Israel. At eighteen years old he was sent to Israel to study electronics, married a young doctor there, and had never returned to Ethiopia. "It has been twenty-five years. I am very moved." Liberally armed with medicine, our new friend supplied Bill with pills for his persistent sinus headache.

For two days Bill and I visited the churches, and when I would tire, Bill would return again and again. They are amazing, and one is inclined to believe the story that the Templar Knights helped in their twelfth-century construction. Bill was particularly fascinated by a Latin cross over one of the arches at the Church of

Mary, a Latin cross surrounded by stars of David. "It seems amazing to me that this small African country became the meeting place of the three great religions of the world."

King Lalibela was actually born in Lalibela (then called Roha) around 1140 A.D. He seemed to have always been destined for greatness. King Lalibela's older half-brother, Harbay, administered a deadly poison to Lalibela that plunged the young man into a cataleptic sleep. During the three days of his sleep it was claimed that Lalibela was transported by angels to the first, second, and third heavens, where he was addressed by the Almighty, who told him to flee Ethiopia and seek refuge in Jerusalem. He was further told "it was his destiny to build a number of wonderful churches in his birthplace the like of which the world had never seen." God then gave Lalibela detailed instructions as to the method of construction, the form that each of the churches was to take, their locations and even their interior and exterior decorations. (For me it is like reading about Moses and his instructions from God.) But about 1160 A.D. --Lalibela would have been about twenty years old. Harbay had him exiled to Jerusalem. Twenty-five years later, in 1185, Lalibela returned to his own country and proclaimed himself king.

In fulfillment of his vision, the new king immediately set about building the eleven spectacular monolithic churches--churches literally carved out of solid volcanic rock. (UNESCO recently declared these churches to be one of the wonders of the world.) In many ways Lalibela tried to recreate Jerusalem. He named the river running through Roha-Lalibela the Jordan, and one of his churches, Beta Golgotha, was specifically designed to symbolize the Church of the Holy Sepulcher in Jerusalem. "Mom, did you know that in medieval times Ethiopia was the only non-European Christian kingdom that existed anywhere in the world?" Bill had not idly majored in history at Stanford University. Our days in Lalibela were deeply nostalgic for me.

So onward north we flew in our green and yellow plane, on to Axum where heads of the Ethiopia's state are crowned. This ancient city is located on the plain of Hazebo, nestled between Mt. Libanos and Mt. Zohodo. It is the site of a civilization so ancient that its antecedents are unknown--the sources of its inspiration unremembered. Regarded at its zenith as one of the great kingdoms of the world, it remains for Ethiopians the heart of their kingdom.

Within an hour of our arrival Bill and I stood outside the Church of St. Mary of Zion in Axum. "Incredible to think that Moses' stone inscribed with the Ten Commandments is said to live inside that church. I guess that is why Axum is so important to the Ethiopians."

"The very center of their Christianity. Oh Bill, I wish we were here for the Epiphany on January 6, when they bring the tablets out to show the faithful." We began a conversation with the old priest guarding the door of the St. Mary of Zion church. The priest was dressed in various layers of clothing in a rainbow of colors. He stood holding a large bronze cross supported by a wooden pole. "The church," he told us, "with its precious tablets inside, is never without a guard." I'm sure that the priest did not know how ancient the town's history real was, although he did ask us if we had seen the stelae. "No, but we're going there now." He bowed his head to us several times, in true Ethiopian courtesy. "They are very old, our stelae, very old."

Historically, Axum was probably founded during the first century B.C. and reached its zenith between the third and fifth centuries A.D. Its lifeline was the caravan route that passed from Adulis on the Red Sea, through

Axum, and on to the Nile and Egypt. In the third century, Mani, an Arab historian, placed the Axumite kingdom among the four greatest empires of that time which included: Babylon, Rome, and Egypt.

Most of the existing remains are attributed to the time of Axum's greatest glory. It was then that the great stelae were constructed, huge stone monoliths that could have been hewn, adorned and erected only with the skills of a great civilization. "Bill, that main stele looks exactly like the Washington monument in Washington D. C. Builders must have used the Axum stele as inspiration."

Besides the main stele lies another that fell more than a thousand years ago. Actually Queen Yoditi, a Jewish Queen of the tenth century, destroyed it. The field next to the daddy stele is filled with small stelae. No historian has been able to discover exactly when they were built and for what purpose, though there are chambers in the bottom of the large stele, perhaps for burial of kings.

At our hotel that night there were only two other travelers in the dining room, not counting a Swiss tour group. These were two ladies about my age and, over Bill's protest, I began a conversation. One of the women turned out to be Susan Belgrave, great granddaughter of the man who was the second in command to Napier when he made his famous excursion into Ethiopia in 1868. We sat long over our coffee talking about our experiences--especially theirs as they had just come off a long mule trip in the highlands.

Our last day came, and after a fine omelet filled with fiery-hot pieces of green pepper, we took a taxi and headed for the airport. Waiting for the plane Bill suddenly shouted, "I left all the clothes that I sent to the hotel laundry!" Jumping in a cab, he headed back up the winding road. Since the planes change schedule by the hour, and our plane had arrived shortly after Bill left, I was in a quandary. Minutes before take-off, the taxi, Bill, and his clothes swooped onto the field. "I would have waited had you not made it, Bill".

"Let's stay our last night in Addis at the Hilton, Bill. John and I were here for its opening night on 6 December 1969." As we walked into the lobby I was in shock seeing the handsome rose-red rug in the center of the lobby. I had forgotten that nearly thirty years ago I had so loved that rug that John and I had two of them made for our home. It took five girls many months to make those thick tufted rugs, and the red one still graces the living room of my log house. The gold one is in my bedroom.

Leaving my writing in the tower room of my log house, I walk to the balcony above my living room and look down at that magnificent red rug, as beautiful as the day we brought it home to our stone house in Addis. And I thought, imagine all the thousands of people who have trod that rug's sister as they pass through the lobby of the Addis Ababa Hilton! And their rug is still in pretty good shape, too! I'll bet my grandchildren will be fighting over my rug-a legacy from the highlands of Ethiopia and a remarkable period in my life.

Index